From Kindertransport to Post-war Sweden

LUCIE WIDL

From Kindertransport to Post-war Sweden: My Memories

Edited with an introduction
by Norbert Götz

Södertörn University

The Institute of Contemporary History /
Samtidshistoriska institutet (SHI)
Södertörns högskola
SE-141 89 Huddinge

www.sh.se/shi

Stockholm 2025

Issues of Contemporary History /
Samtidshistoriska frågor 50
ISSN: 2004-8858
ISBN: 978-91-89615-50-2

Contents

Introduction to Lucie Widl's Memoir

Lucie Widl, born Lucie Hilsenrad on 2 January 1930 in Vienna, had a long life, but it was not all easy. When she passed away on 16 February 2023 in Stockholm at age ninety-three, she had been ill for years. This memoir brings her back in vigorous health – full of sharp observations, trenchant comments, laconic humour, and hopeful aspirations. Relatives and friends recited major parts of this manuscripit at a memorial ceremony on 4 June 2023 on the island of Ingarö, Sweden. Afterwards participants asked for copies either for themselves, or to give or read to their children.

I attended the ceremony and found Lucie Widl's narrative compelling and worthy of a broader audience. There is no finer memorial for her than these, her own words. However, this is more than a personal story or a memorial in honour of a recently deceased individual. The narrative published here is entitled *From Kindertransport to Post-war Sweden: My Memories*. It provides an account on the margins of the Holocaust that is embedded in the timeline of the twentieth century, traversing European borders and with linkeages beyond. It illustrates the human condition in a historical context that intersects with the present. Lucie Widl's perspective is authentic and genuine. Although she did not conceive of this manuscript in terms beyond her immediate family circle, her account forcefully raises universal issues that call for engagement by the wider public.

Lucie's childhood in Vienna was overshadowed by the Great Depression. By 1938 the German Reich's incorporation of Austria imposed the terror of the Nazis onto her life. As a family with one Jewish spouse and a Jewish family orientation, Lucie's parents were quick to send their two children on a 1939 *Kindertransport* (child transport) to Scotland. Lucie and her sister were among roughly 10,000 unaccompanied refugee minors who arrived in the United Kingdom before the beginning of the Second World War.

The relatively safe environment came at the price of a childhood without parents, and Lucie's account confirms the increasingly critical research on the Kindertransport scheme that did not provide a refuge for adults or families.[1] The Kindertransport literature is extensive, consisting both of accounts by those who experienced it and academic research. Lucie's memoir is a contribution that addresses 'the forgotten Kindertransportees', as the displaced children who were sent to Scotland have been called.[2]

In post-war London, still as a refugee minor, Lucie experienced how differently relatives and friends assumed responsibility for her. She was fortunate that her father was among the roughly 5,000 Jews who survived the Holocaust in Vienna.[3] However, a gap had emerged between her and her parents that proved difficult to bridge upon her return. Her new cosmopolitan life phase brought engagement with a partner from Sweden and ended with separation from him a few years later.

The last third of Lucie's memoir describes the establishment of a new intimate relationship and the foundation of a family, still in Sweden, but now within a distinct community of immigrants from various German-speaking countries. Personal issues move into the foreground in this part of the narrative, and annotations by the editor become more infrequent, but this does not affect the broader validity. Instead, this shift reflects priorities across the human life cycle and the arrival of calmer, more peaceful times. In addition, Lucie's experiences as a mother brought her in more than usual contact with medical facilities. Her account of this highlights the workings of Swedish welfare institutions in the 1960s and onwards. Her family received excellent care at reasonable cost.

A question that arises is Lucie Widl's 'Jewishness'. Those who knew her recall her as an outspoken atheist, something the memoir reflects. She was born to a mother from a Catholic family background and to a Jewish father, thus not qualifying as Jewish in accordance with a Jewish principle of matrilineal descent. However, Lucie was not baptised as a child. Rather, she was registered with the Jewish Community of Vienna and given a second Hebrew name, Ruth (Rut).[4] She was treated as Jewish in Austria by the end of the 1930s. According to the Nazi conception of a national community, as codified in the Nuremberg racial laws, she was half-Jewish, a category that was subject to varying degrees of discrimination and persecution in different realms of Nazi authority.[5] The definition of British refugee organisations acknowledged this fact. They regarded a 'Jew' as anyone affected by the Nuremberg laws.[6] It is also indicative that Lucie's parents decided to send her away on a Kindertransport. In the years that followed, she was involved in Jewish educational schemes in the United Kingdom. Apparently, Lucie conceived herself as being essentially of Jewish heritage, her Swedish fiancee perceived her as Jewish, and when she finally married a Catholic, she acquiesced as a necessary formality to undergo a religious conversion procedure. Overall, her account reflects a Jewish experience.

Little is known about the history of the memoir itself, it's evolution and time of writing. We do know that Lucie's husband, Walter Widl, encouraged her to write her life story. She drafted the manuscript in English, the language she had acquired during her formative years in the United Kingdom, and with which she remained most comfortable reading and writing throughout her lifetime. She composed the manuscript that this publication is based upon on a personal computer, designating it as Version two. No previous draft has been preserved. The mention in the text of a chessboard given to Lucie's oldest grandchild shows that it was finalised not earlier than 2007. However, it is possible that it is based on an earlier draft that might date as far back as the 1990s or perhaps even the 1980s.

The memoir's original title is 'Lucie's memories'. Section captions that highlight the structure of the manuscript have been added, and the text has been edited slightly on a few occasions to improve its format and legibility for a broader audience. Annotations, such as translations, biographical and other types of information, and quotations from complementary literature have been added in footnotes. The manuscript was found in a portfolio that did not include other materials.

For this publication, additional photographs and documents from private and public sources have been identified and included. Most significant is Lucie Hilsenrad's case file, which is preserved in the World Jewish Relief (formerly Central British Fund) Archives. Some gaps in the memoir's narrative were impossible to resolve with the available sources and in the time available. My hope is nevertheless that Holocaust and migration education, on the one hand, and researchers dealing with the Holocaust, Kindertransport, and migration, on the other, will find Lucie Widl's memoir a significant, first-hand account in their respective fields.

Without Arvid and Alexandra Widl's kind sharing of Lucie Widl's manuscript and other materials, this publication would not have been possible. Adrian Rösiö has generously contributed photographs that document Lucie's life around 1950. Various archives have provided material that corroborate the narrative. I owe special thanks to Harvey Kaplan, Director of the Scottish Jewish Archives Centre, and to Susanne Uslu-Pauer, Director of the Archive of the Jewish Community of Vienna. The Institute of Contemporary History at Södertörn University in Stockholm has provided me with the infrastructure neccessary to produce this book, including research time supported by funding from the Foundation for Baltic and East European Studies. The Institute of Contemporary History has included the manuscript in the series *Issues of Contemporary History / Samtidshistoriska frågor*, the focus of which is the publication of new and untapped sources for research, based on accounts given by contemporary witnesses. The Södertörn University Library has also generously contributed to the production of this book in various ways. My sincere gratitude to all of them!

Norbert Götz
Stockholm, January 2025

*This memoir covers the most critical years of my life.
I dedicate these lines to my beloved children and family
who made my life worth living.*

1. Childhood in Austria

My mother's family was Catholic,[1] and my father's family was Jewish;[2] it was a mixed marriage.[3] We celebrated Christmas, but also Chanuka and Purim. There was great tolerance in the family as far as religion was concerned. Only vague memories of my childhood remain. Where shall I begin?

Before my sister Margit[4] was born in 1927, both our parents worked together in the pharmacy on Stephansplatz in Vienna, Austria.[5] Mother was the cashier and took care of wages etc. It was always a huge treat to visit my father when he was on night duty. All these bottles and tiny drawers full of poison. In those days *Papa* made all the pills by hand, including many creams and lotions. He experimented a lot and managed to find formulas for many 'beauty products', which did not induce allergies, something almost unheard of at that time. Unfortunately, he lost a lot of money during the Wall Street crash.[6] As I was born in 1930, it probably explains mother's comment: 'you were not a wanted child'. From what my father told me, I was a very lively child with lots of friends. At one point the parents contacted my teacher as I never seemed to have any homework. Five minutes before I was sent to bed I 'remembered' what I had to do for school the next day. Margit was often told to help me, in order to get me off to bed. She must have resented this. She was regarded to be a genius, which did her great harm in later years.[7] As far as I remember, she was always a fairly lonely child. As my reports from school were inevitably good, the parents eventually calmed down.

The summers were mostly spent in St. Jakob in Kärnten[8] together with Tante Joscha, Mother's younger sister, and my cousin Susi from Vienna. It was always a huge upheaval before we left town. Everything had to be taken along, including pots and pans. Sheets were draped over the furniture and huge suitcases and baskets were finally loaded on the train. Papa always remained in

Fig. 1. Ludwig and Maria Hilsenrad, 1931 (courtesy of Alexandra Widl).

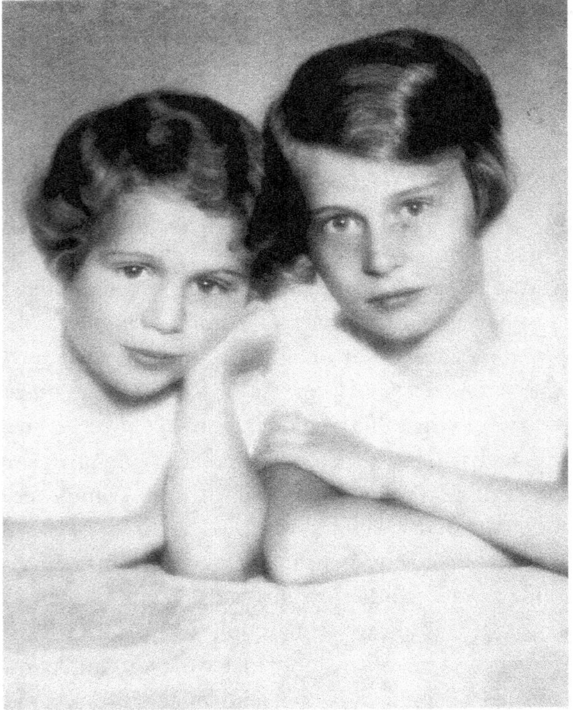

Fig. 2. Lucie Hilsenrad (l.) and sister Margit in Vienna, 1930s
(Photo: Atelier Willi Pollak;[9] courtesy of Alexandra Widl).

town and only came out to visit us for a few weeks. I guess in those days one had very little 'official' holiday. He was definitely a 'town person', so this arrangement suited him well.

A trauma from Kärnten, even to this day, is my terrible fear of snakes, thanks to Margit who got some locals to catch some harmless snakes. She put the snakes in my bed at night. There was also a near drowning incident when I was five years old in a forest swimming pool with muddy ground and unclear water. No one saw me disappear and after what seemed an eternity, I reached the deepest end and caught hold of a ladder. Needless to say, I could not swim and must have practiced the same tactics that dogs use. It was a sheer miracle that I survived, and I am still today not very happy when surrounded by lots of deep water. My mother gave me a good thrashing because I got my hair wet. When she realised what had happened, I got some ice cream! Margit tried to teach me how to swim the following year on our parquet floor with the result that a big splinter pierced my leg which had to be cut out. I still have a six-inches scar as a souvenir of that lesson.

I only went to school for two years in Vienna before leaving for England. By chance, I still have my 'school' and 'character' report from one of my teachers and even a photo with all my classmates. I am the tiny tot in the middle holding the slate. How these things survived the war is a mystery.[10]

Fig. 3. 'Lucie [holding the slate] in primary school in Meidling', 1937 (Meidling being the 12th district of Vienna) (courtesy of Alexandra Widl).

The parents had to move fourteen times during the war, some-times bombed out, sometimes evicted. On the first occasion, Margit and I were still in Vienna. Some Nazis wanted our flat so we had to move out on the double.[11] Fear in the air, fear: 'will Papa come home safe in the evening', fear all around us.[12] Crystal Night, 10 November 1938,[13] Vienna's sky painted red, the parents whispering. Margit was suddenly sent to Onkel Poldi and Tante Mina in Klosterneuburg with money and jewellery. She was only ten years old; it was already evening and ten kilometres away. She must have been terrified. Tante Mina, mother's older sister, and Onkel Poldi, a building contractor, lived in a house in Klosterneuburg with a garden full of fruit trees. The old chessboard, which we gave to [our grandson] Linus belonged to Onkel Poldi. Both loved the children as they had none of their own; their only child died as a baby. It was always a great treat to spend the weekend with them.

My grandmother Rosa had three daughters: Maria (my mother), Mina, and Joscha. The diamond ring I often wear is a legacy from my grandmother, who gave it to her eldest daughter, Tante Mina, who saved it for me. Tante Mina told me later that Tante Joscha was furious about this as she wanted the ring for her daughter Susie. She had made a remark to the effect: 'the Hilsenrad girls won't survive the war anyway'.

My grandmother Rosa[14] came from a family of *Perlensticker*, that is, embroidering in pearls, the hight of fashion at this time. She settled in Meidling after emigrating from Czechoslovakia. She often loved to go to the theatre and with a lace shawl on her head she got into her carriage and off she went on her own. Rosa tried to commit suicide once and landed in a psychiatric ward for many years – during this period my mother was still young. My grand-father came to Vienna from Slovakia as a boy with bare hands.[15] Within a few years, however, he had his own store and later still was classified as a *nobel Hausbesitzer*[16] with a number of servants etc. Seemingly my grandfather was a real tyrant and once he threw some acid at his wife Rosa and missed her. However, my mother, who was in the bathroom with her on this occasion, got the full force of the acid on her bottom, and to the end of her life she had scars. During the absence of the mother the three sisters were thus left alone with a very strict father. Some of this definitely seems to have rubbed off on my mother and Tante Joscha. I do not remember ever getting a hug or praise for anything I ever did at home. Tante Mina was different; she was the sort of story book auntie whom all the children adored. A lot of our furniture was stored in their house during the war and, due to this, was spared.

Near the end of the war my mother sat in prison for a year for saying in a milk queue in our local store: 'I hope Hitler dies soon'. Hitler was seemingly ill at this time. Fifteen minutes later, they fetched her after being denounced by someone in the queue.[17] She had great civil courage and [when in prison] managed to keep everyone's spirits up. By saving breadcrumbs she made an entire chess set and taught the inmates of her cell how to play chess. She also formed an orchestra simply by placing a piece of paper over a comb, the perfect instrument if you have nothing. Papa obtained no food coupons during this period, and it must have been very difficult for him, but both survived. Sadly enough, Papa became blind after being forced to work on weaving mats without sufficient light.[18] They almost got him at the very end when men who were the last remnants of mixed marriages were herded together at the railway station, to be sent to Auschwitz. Luckily the transports had broken down, nothing was working anymore, and he was sent home.[19]

2. Kindertransport experience

One day we were politely told that we were no longer welcome at the local school in Vienna. Next scene is at the railway station.[20] Hundreds of children, Red Cross nurses everywhere and all around us parents, some forcing smiles on their faces, some openly crying. I was seven-and-a-half and Margit ten years old. I could not understand what was happening, nobody explained. So, we left Vienna and our parents.[21] After a very long journey we landed in Scotland.[22] Some of the children were taken to Holland, some to Paris, never to be heard of again. This happened to a distant cousin of ours, also called Lucie and of my age.[23]

We[24] came to a very wealthy family called Morrison, who had two children of their own, roughly our age.[25] At the outbreak of the war, it gave great status to families who took in 'refugees'. Unfortunately, they treated us rather badly compared with their own children. For instance, we were not allowed to go to their private school but had to go to a local one; nor were we allowed to take

4350

This document of identity is issued with the approval of His Majesty's Government in the United Kingdom to young persons to be admitted to the United Kingdom for educational purposes under the care of the Inter-Aid Committee for children.

THIS DOCUMENT REQUIRES NO VISA.

PERSONAL PARTICULARS.

2315

Name HILSENRAD LUZIE

Sex F   Date of Birth 2. . 30

Place VIENNA

Full Names and Address of Parents

HILSENRAD, LUDWIG, MARIE

65, SIEBENBRUNNENGALLE

VIENNA 5

Fig. 4. Lucie's UK visa waiver document, 1939 (courtesy of World Jewish Relief [formerly Central British Fund] Archives).

part in the private French lessons for their children at home, despite the fact that we knew as much or more than they did, thanks to our private French teacher in Vienna. This was obviously not very popular, as we were supposed to be second class 'citizens'.[26] From the first day on we were forbidden to talk German (as was the case in the whole of England). As a result, I forgot my 'mother tongue' within the first year but could speak fluent English after six months. In the beginning it made us feel even more homesick and lonely, as Margit and I could no longer communicate in German, leaving us no language at all for the first initial months. Margit's braces on her teeth were removed and the treatment discontinued as it was 'too expensive'.[27] This from a family who bought a genuine Stradivarius for the father, an amateur hobby fiddler at home.[28] Tom, the chauffeur, took pity on us and sometimes drove us to or fetched us from school in the family Bentley. It was the unhappiest time in my life.

In the end Margit asked the family 'to send us away'. Where on Earth to? Our parents had their passports taken away, so we knew that at best we would not see them again until the end of the war. That is how we landed in several children homes for refugees.[29] During the war one could write a so-called Red Cross Letter, consisting of twenty-five words. Margit wrote dozens of them during the nine years that we were on our own. None of them ever reached the parents.

We were about eighty children in Skelmorlie, a real Scottish *kråkslott*,[30] sleeping six to eight, sometimes even more people, in a dormitory. Obviously, we had no bicycles, so in rain or sunshine we had to walk to school. The school was rather far away, as the castle was situated in a huge park in the midst of nowhere. On Saturdays, we were all lined up to have our hair examined for lice. Then followed the weekly bath and our hair was washed with carbolic soap, which smelled ghastly. Near the end of our stay there I caught scarlet fever. The children were very happy because they were all put into quarantine, meaning no school! They took me to hospital where I lost most of my hair and became stone deaf

Fig. 5. Potato peeler, sketch by Lucie Hilsenrad, 1943. From the Irene & Ernst Marchand Collection, Scottish Jewish Archives Centre (PER.Marchand/0003/22). Copyright and not to be reproduced without permission. – Irene Marchand was a refugee from Gelsenkirchen, Germany, who served as a cook and matron of various Scottish hostels.

for three months. As Penicillin was practically unknown and, as a matter of fact, was just in the process of being tested on wounded soldiers, I had little chance of getting real help.

When I returned, I found that Skelmorlie was almost disbanded and that some of us were sent to a children home near Edinburgh called Ernespie, another Scottish castle.[31] Margit and I were separated. She was sent to Glasgow to continue her schooling. There she took her matriculation exam as well as a course in secretarial work.[32]

Ernespie was different in so far as the place was run on the same principles as a Kibbutz, called *hachshara*.[33] We were prepared for life in a Kibbutz. We were about eighty children between the ages of thirteen and twenty years. We had a big vegetable garden and about a thousand chickens. Food was scarce, so everything we produced was important. We used a rotating working scheme, which changed once a month. Either one did the laundry (for eighty people without a washing machine) or one worked in the kitchen, the garden, or with the chickens. In addition, we had to mind all the other things, such as mending clothes, shoes and what not. We were given clean working clothes now and then. In school I sewed a dress for myself which was my most precious possession for years. We had no money of our own. Not even our birthdays were celebrated, let alone receiving a present from someone. One hour before school and each afternoon we had to work at our chores. With the exception of Saturday, we never got a day off.

At the end of the war, I was put on the working list as 'nurse'.[34] For some odd reason I was kept on this job for many months looking after eighty people with cuts and bruises, sore throats etc. In serious cases I called the village doctor, a kind old man who taught me a lot.

Without any warning, ten Auschwitz survivors were sent to us during this period of chaos in Europe. Some brainy person obviously thought we would be a good rehabilitation centre for these children. Needless to say, they hated us on sight. After all they had been through, they were certainly not willing to do any work whatsoever. What they needed was a psychologist with whom they could talk to about some of their traumatic experiences.

As they were in very poor health, I often came in contact with them in my capacity as 'nurse'. I even managed to gain some of their trust and confidence. For example, we could not explain the disappearance of bread from the breakfast table each morning. In the end I found the bread hidden under their mattresses. As there were lots of mice in the castle, this was a problem. It took a long time for them to understand that there would always be bread for breakfast, the next day and the next ...[35]

Despite the chaos, the Red Cross did its utmost trying to re-unite family members, in particular trying to find surviving relatives to all the refuge children in Britain. Out of eighty children in Ernespie only one other boy, Margit, and I found our parents again. Some found distant relatives in Australia and the USA, but no parents. Many decades later we passed in New Zealand a farm selling vegetables called Ernespie. I realised too late it could have been someone from our children's home in England.

One day we were told to stand in line and two complete strangers from the refugee committee decided on our fate. I had two choices as I had just finished primary school and not yet entered a *gymnasium*:[36] to become farmer or dressmaker.[37] Obviously, I chose dressmaking, thinking even at this stage, how to sew will always come in useful. But I was devastated knowing that my primary school education was all I was to get for many years to come. Many of us had parents with an academic background and we all realised how different our lives would have been if the families had not been split up because of the war. One boy became insane, one committed suicide, we all became very depressed.[38]

3. Post-war life in London

Moving to London was a big step. I was placed in an orthodox 'woman's hostel', which meant that all the rituals of Sabbath etc. had to be followed. This clashed badly with my lifestyle as the weekend was the only time I had for cultural activities.[39]

The Charouxs,[40] good family friends from Vienna, often gave wonderful dinners for friends on Saturday evenings. As they had more or less adopted me, I was always invited. I met the most fantastic and interesting people. One incident I will never forget.

Fig. 6. Austrian born British artist and sculptor Siegfried Charoux (1896–1967) at work in his studio in England on 31 January 1946 (Photo by Erich Auerbach/Popperfoto via Getty Images).

When Furtwängler[41] came to the Royal Albert Hall for the first time after the war, the tickets were sold out immediately. Margit Charoux[42] phoned me on the day of the concert and told me to be there straight after work. She gave me a sandwich and a ticket belonging to David Astor (one time owner of the newspaper *Observer*).[43] I sat in a magnificent stall surrounded by very elegant people. David in contrast joined the Charouxs high up in the gallery, a fantastic gesture! I was shy, clumsy, fifteen years old, but by listening and observing, my 'education' progressed by leaps and bounds. Incidentally, during the war people in Austria heard Charoux's voice when they listened illegally to the BBC news broadcasted from London. After the war the Viennese made him Professor at the Kunstakademie[44] and erected a special museum on the outskirts of Vienna to house his sculptures and paintings.[45] Sadly enough, he contracted cancer and did not live to be present at the inauguration. Margit Charoux spent the rest of her life trying to round up most of his works. These two kind and gifted persons have influenced my life and my way of thinking more than anyone in the world and I am still eternally grateful to them, especially for the moral support and love they gave me at a time when I needed it most.

We were enrolled in a handicraft school 'ORT' where I learned the art of 'haute couture', that is, to sew, cut, and make pattern.[46] After that I worked in an atelier in Knightsbridge.[47] A dressmaker meets many neurotic rich clients, some of them real beasts. My most interesting experience there was an order for an evening dress for the actress Natalie Wood[48] at the Ealing Film Studio. She was too busy to come into town, so I went out to the Studio for each fitting. I was more than nervous.

During my stay in London, I finally met Phoebus and Olly Tuttnauer,[49] who emigrated to England in 1938. He was Papa's cousin from Romania and my father paid for his entire medical studies in Vienna. He took all of Papa's formulas to England. He opened a laboratory where the lotions and creams were produced by his brother, and he used these products in his flourishing practice as dermatologist. He was the worst snob imaginable and

Fig. 7. 'Self-Portrait' by Phoebus Tuttnauer, 1959 (Tate Archive, © Estate of Richard Gainsborough).

on his piano were signed portraits of all the famous people he had treated from the royal family downwards. He never lifted a finger to help us![50] If Margit and I had been given a small percentage of his profit, a sort of royalty on Papa's inventions, we would have been quite well off. He was talented in many ways and even managed to make a name for himself as an artist creating naivist sketches and paintings.[51]

On 8 June 1949, before I turned twenty-one years,[52] I decided to acquire British citizenship as a minor.[53] It was a one-time offer for refugees who had spent the war in Britain. The naturalisation paper equals to having been born in the country (Nationality Act 1948). Margit retained her Austrian citizenship as she was past the age limit and wanted to return to Vienna at all cost.

4. Travels and engagement

Fig. 8. Vienna Peace Institute, Lucie Hilsenrad 4th from the right, on her right her sister Margit (*Gospel Messenger* 99 (9 Dec. 1950), p. 19).[54]

My first short visit to Vienna was a strange experience.[55] Margit had returned the year before and was working for an American relief agency.[56] Meeting the parents for the first time after so many years was difficult.[57] I had left them as a child and was now grown up. We were strangers to each other, quite apart that I could not speak a word of German.[58] On my second visit I stayed for six months.[59] I took a course in a very high-brow academy for dressmakers, tailors, and haute couture. Picking up rudimentary German went rather fast. However, there was no work to be had in postwar Vienna. I quickly found out that it would be impossible to live at home again. Thanks to all we had gone through on our own in England, we had become mature far beyond our age. A fact the parents could not cope with. Margit lived with a distant aunt, Tante Toni, and there was no room for all of us in her flat. Tante Toni's husband illustrated the Austrian craving for titles.

When I first met Onkel Jules I was told to call him *Staatsbahnrat*. He waved this away and said, 'if anything I am an *Oberstaatsbahnrat*'.[60] We finally settled on 'Onkel Jules', which was easier.

The International Club in Vienna was a blessing. There one could speak English and meet all sorts of people of different nationalities. There I met Bengt, a Swede, who had just finished his studies.[61]

Before returning to England, we, that is, Bengt, a Swedish girl and I, made a marvellous trip to Marocco, Algeria, Tunisia, Portugal, Spain, and Andorra. It took three months and was probably one of the first interrail journeys possible. In Morocco we travelled fourth class on top of buses and hired bicycles to go from Marrakesh to the various oases. One could travel everywhere without fear, very little money was needed to get us through. We girls were even allowed to visit a real harem, quite an experience to meet these women in their golden cage. A far cry from the scenes Holywood tried to portray. They were virtually prisoners, kidnapped when they were very young girls. Tourists were as yet practically unknown. In some places in the Atlas Mountains, we were the first 'white' visitors to enter tiny villages, despite the fact that the French Foreign Legion was everywhere.[62]

Finally, back in Paris we met a bus full of academic film enthusiasts, most of them Bengt's student friends from Sweden, among others Billy Klüver.[63] All borders were finally open, and they were on their way to the most famous cinematheques in Europe. As a result of this meeting, I was invited to Sweden and celebrated Christmas in Sälen. Billy Klüver's father owned the hotel.[64] It was an interesting crowd. Among others Pontus Hultén who since then has installed many museums of modern art worldwide.[65]

After six months in Stockholm in 1949, I went to Paris as an au-pair and Bengt attended the Sorbonne for advanced studies, which were necessary when entering the foreign office.[66] We became engaged, but after five years we broke it off. We had simply grown apart and had developed in completely different directions, without common interests.[67] He was posted to India where he got married to an English girl, whom he divorced a few years later. In time, he became Ambassador and many years later I figured in one of his books. He compared the break-up to Arthur Köstler, who threw all his medical books over a bridge, the day he wanted to start a new life and became a writer.[68]

Fig. 9. Lucie at Jemaa El-Fnaa Square, Marrakesh, Spring 1950 (courtesy of Adrian Rösiö).

Fig. 10. Bus of Bengt's friends, to be carried on a ferry across the English Channel (with unidentified man), 1950 (courtesy of Adrian Rösiö).

Fig. 11. Farewell from Lucie's fiancée, 1953 (l. Lucie Hilsenrad, centre Bengt Rösiö, r. unknown woman) (courtesy of Adrian Rösiö).

5. Sweden in the 1950s

On my return to Stockholm, after Paris, I worked in two different ateliers in Östermalm.[69] It was easy to get a working permit in those days. However, it was a very unpleasant and sad experience. In the evenings I went to night school, Påhlmans Handelsinstitut, where I took a secretarial course in English and Swedish short-hand, typing, business correspondence, and a German language course. Thanks to this I got in 1952 a good job at Grängesbergs-bolaget on Gustav Adolfs Torg.[70] Cecily,[71] a good friend of mine, worked in the SE Bank,[72] located in the next building. My English came in very handy as Grängesberg was handling the huge con-tracts with Liberia resulting in the LAMCO project, one of the largest open cast iron mines developed at that time.[73] It was a very interesting work, which included everything from planning, housing, and schools for the natives, including shipping problems and miles of translations. I remained with the firm until 1962.

We were paid a fairly low wage compared to what one earns nowadays, but I could save enough to go to Vienna at Christmas each year. On one of those trips, I met Walter.[74] Due to heavy snow the trains were delayed, and we missed our connections. We met in the same first-class compartment (with second-class tickets) on the train from Copenhagen to the ferry. In the storm on the ferry over to Germany I was seasick, and Walter came over to me as I stood by the railing and asked the idiotic question: 'Fräulein, können Sie kochen?'[75] A madman on the loose? We once again landed in the same train by chance and Walter using his railroad key reserved a compartment just for the two of us. Walter proceeded to take out his alarm clock, put on his pyjamas on top of all his other clothes, and went to sleep. It convinced me that he was a complete lunatic on leave. Many months later I got a note from him via the British Embassy, asking me if I would like to go to a concert with him. He had seemingly copied my name and address from my suitcase.

In 1956 my friend Eva Nobel, whom I met in my German course at Påhlmans, invited us out to their mansion in Nynäshamn.[76] Her mother, a Russian princess, wanted to scrutinise Walter. I had visited them once before, so I knew what was coming. The only thing I could say to Walter was 'Be yourself' and we spent a lovely weekend picking mushrooms. Before we left, we were given a bottle of sherry from 1917, to be drunk on a special occasion.

6. Marriage

That summer we met Walter's parents, his brother Gerhard and Renate in Austria to spend a week together. One day we went for a hike up the Jufen mountain top, near Millstadt in Kärnten.

Walter and Opa[77] kept lagging more and more behind, planning something. I got really suspicious when Opa started picking *Enzian*[78] near the summit as he was not exactly the flower picking type. It was a beautiful day with a magnificent view and Walter could not have chosen a better and more romantic spot for our engagement.

In order to marry Walter, I had to convert to Catholicism, which was in itself an ordeal. Luckily the Dutch priest who initiated us and taught us the rites and rules of the Catholic church, was a fantastic person. We and the three other converts in our group adored Dr Mirlov. He was a real *Mensch*,[79] no absurd holiness nor hypocrisy, just very humane. I told him that I would never go to confession nor to church every Sunday as I was skeptical to the whole enforced hokus pokus, be it Catholic or Jewish. He understood me completely and merely made a comment to the effect that it was far more healthy to go for a long walk than sit indoors. This comment coming from a vice bishop! We wanted him to perform our wedding in Stuttgart, which he would have loved to do. Being the person he was, he had ignored his pains for months, which sadly turned out to be advanced cancer, and he died within a few weeks.

The civil ceremony took place in Stockholm's Rådhuset in December 1957.[80] Evi and Max Gugolz were our witnesses.[81] We all worked until lunch and went straight to the Rådhuset from the office. The whole ceremony was over in five minutes. The officiant merely shook hands and said: 'May I congratulate you, that will be three kronor' all in one breath and turning his hand for the coins. It could hardly have been less romantic. We had a little dinner at my place on Gärdet after the ceremony. I even remember making Wiener Schnitzel with Evi in the kitchen. In those days restaurants were too expensive for all of us. Walter lived in Högdalen until we were properly married a few weeks later, as it was like in the fifties.

The church wedding took place in a little chapel in Stuttgart, two days before Christmas. My father was not present as he was already too ill to travel. I really regretted his absence. It would have been marvelous to have his support instead of my mother's comment as I was dressing for the ceremony: 'Is Walter not too young for you?'[82] Unfortunately, but well meaning, Opa made all the arrangements, and any discussion was out of question. His idea of a good plan was: first the wedding, Christmas with the whole family, then a one-day honeymoon in a huge deserted hotel in the Black Forest village Liebeszell,[83] where we were the only guests.

He even managed to squeeze in an invitation to lunch in Karlsruhe at his sister Dora's and husband Edi's flat the day before the ceremony. The Fiebichs had forgotten to put on the heating in the dining room and we were expected to sit down and enjoy a meal in 15 degrees.[84] So, I fetched my coat, which shocked Oma[85] and Opa (five minutes later, both put on their coats). The Fiebichs once visited us in Ingarö. Martin Ljung's 'Ester' summons up the situation.[86]

Before we left Stockholm, Walter had signed a five-year contract with a firm called ALWAC in California. Among the 'good luck' telegrammes, which we read during our wedding dinner, one telegramme informed Walter that the firm in USA had gone bankrupt. It was difficult to get into a party spirit after that. On our return, Walter joined LM Ericsson and, luckily, I still had my job with Grängesbergsbolaget. In spite of the terrible housing shortage, we managed to get a little flat in Hägersten. The great building boom started first in the sixties, such as Vällingby, Farsta, and many more. Most of the tenants in Hägersten were working class, many with alcoholic problems. Often as not our kitchen window was smashed, so after two years we decided to find something else.

Fig. 12. Wedding, 1957 (courtesy of Alexandra Widl).

By then, the Lockners, Walter's cousin Irma married to Dieter, moved from their one room flat in Döbelnsgatan to a four-room flat in Vedevågsslingan 7 (Högdalen).[87] Lockners had a very tough time, as Dieter was working on his doctoral dissertation at the De Hevesy Institute.[88] Many evenings they ate potatoes and fish, which had been subjected to radioactivity in his experiments. They bought 1966 a nice house in Trångsund. By chance, one of Dieter's colleagues moved to the USA and by giving them some money we got the contract near the Lockner location, Vedevågsslingan 9, a four-room flat on the ninth floor with an amazing view.

7. Building a migrant family and the Swedish healthcare system

Walter and I wanted a family, but after five years we had more or less given up the hope that we would ever have children. In 1961 we left for a wonderful holiday in Majorca. In those days there were few tourists and many beaches without hotels. On our return I found I was pregnant. I was thirty-one years old.

We were very happy, and I continued working as usual. Apart from slight sickness in the mornings the first two months, and now and then a dizzy spell in the underground when the train was packed, I felt fine. Luckily, I did not put on much weight, ten kilos all in all. In fact, when I went around to say goodbye, two months before Arvid was due, many colleagues asked me why I was leaving the firm.

Finally, 'free' at home I started a grand spring cleaning, which accounted probably for Arvid's arrival four weeks premature. As I felt only slight labour pains on 8 June, and despite the fact that most of the fluid had gone, leaving the baby floating in little liquid, the nurse from Södra BB told us to stay at home and take it easy.[89] We played records half the night and finally decided to drive to the hospital at 12 o'clock lunchtime on 9 June. As soon as they realised they had given me wrong instructions on the phone, they treated me as if I was made of porcelain.

After approximately twenty-nine hours in labour, also counting the time at home, Arvid finally arrived at 8:35 in the evening. He was a very little bundle weighing 2190 g and was 45 cm long. Immediately he was whisked off to an incubator and as he caught jaundice on the second day, turning very yellow, he was removed to Karolinska[90] for a possible blood transfusion on account of a rhesus factor. Arvid came back to Södra BB, and I stayed a couple of days with him to improve his weight.

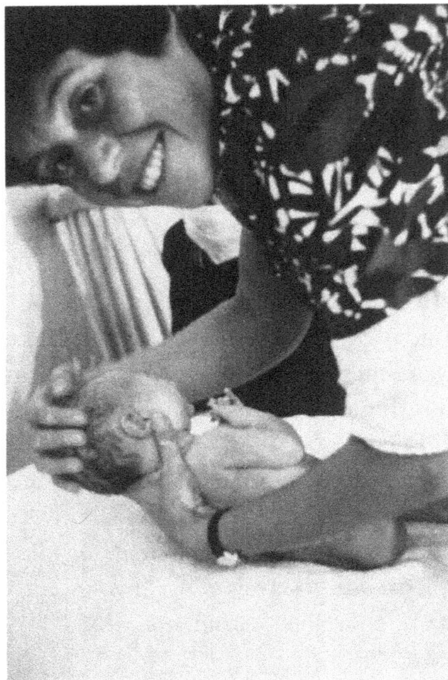

Fig. 13. Lucie with son Arvid, 1962 (courtesy of Alexandra Widl).

Walter's best friend Gerhard Gobl visited me daily as Walter had a business trip to USA.[91] Everybody considered Gerhard as the loving father. When Walter finally returned, I had a lot of explaining to do! Arvid had to have food every four hours. He had lost a lot of weight due to the jaundice and was down to 1.7 kg at his lowest. Later he was removed to Serafen under special care until he recorded 2½ kg when we finally could take him home.[92] But we had not prepared anything in advance. Due to his prolonged stay in hospital, we could shop in peace for his specific needs. He could sleep in a cot first when he was three months old.

On his first visit to town, about two months old, a little girl at NK[93] looked in the carrier bag and said: 'what a sweet little doll' – she honestly thought he was a toy. Dr Blomgren, our wonderful pediatrician, who came day and night whenever our children were ill, advised us to take Arvid south to prolong the summer and get stronger before the dark, harsh Swedish winter arrived. We decided to go to Ascona; Oma and Opa joined us in Switzerland.

Now that we had a family, we thought of two alternatives. Either to buy a house in town, as most of our friends had done, or to keep the flat and buy something near the sea. One day, our friends, the Wagners, made us aware of the fact that there were still some lots to be had in lngarö.[94] We had earlier visited lngarö during weekend excursions and loved the nature and beaches. So, we drove out immediately and we decided to buy the end property adjacent to 10 km of wild forest. Thus, we became neighbours to the Wagners. The decision had to be made fast as there was another client interested in the same lot. We also loved the rock plateau, which seemed the perfect place on which to build the house. It was a big step for us, considering we were living on one salary only.

In the sixties there were still very few public day nurseries available, most of the queue was taken up by social cases. We had no relatives here, so most of us in our circle of friends became housewives when our children were born. Arvid was a quiet child, and it took some time for him to catch up. He crawled eagerly around in the living room and was fascinated by the knobs on the radio, which we had at floor level.

One day he simply stood up, somewhat unsteadily to be sure, and started walking. The same phenomenon took place when he started speaking. On principle we never used 'baby talk' with the children and we decided to speak only German at home. Single words did not seem to interest Arvid. When he finally made up his mind, he spoke whole sentences. On one of our visits, Dr Blomgren discovered that Arvid had a rupture of the hernia. We were whisked off to the children's hospital Kronprincessan Luise and he had an immediate operation. I will never forget Arvid's expression when he thought we were abandoning him to these complete strangers.

When he was about two years old, we prolonged the summer in Seeboden (Austria). On our way down in our VW we stopped in Stuttgart, and Arvid was baptised in the same little chapel in which we were married. Dieter and Margit are his godparents although the church was against it, as neither of them are catholic.

In Seeboden we rented together with Gerhard's family small houses right by the lake with our own waterfront.[95] Oma, Urgrossmutter,[96] and Opa also came to Seeboden and lived in a little *Pension*[97] nearby. On the first day, when we were having breakfast, Opa came marching in and asked us what plans we had for the day. In the same breath he told Renate and me that Oma would not babysit for us, which we had never asked her to do in the first place.

One nice memory I still have from Seeboden is of Urgrossmutter, a tiny bent old lady, coming down to us after breakfast with bread and rolls, to feed the swans. Cousin Ann-Kathrin and Arvid probably ate more of the bread than the swans. They always looked forward to the moment when she came into the garden, and together they went to the lake. One day when I had removed Arvid's swimming pants, as he was more in the water than out of it, a neighbour leaning over the fence objected to him bathing naked. Each morning they went off with small baskets to Penker[98] to fetch fresh rolls for breakfast. Oma would lie in wait to bribe them with chocolate, which spoilt their appetite. All in all, we spent three wonderful autumns together in Seeboden, the last two with three children: Ann-Kathrin, Arvid, and Tienchen. We enjoyed swimming, hiking, and good food, often fetched from a nearby hotel.

By the spring of 1964 we had finally saved enough money and after contacting a building constructor, he began with a team of four to build the *stuga*[99] in Ingarö. It was finished by the summer and all that was left was paintwork, electricity, and water installations. Easier said than done. In those days we had to fetch the water from a communal hand-activated pump, about a 100 m down the road. In the kitchen we had an AGA stove heated by wood, which we had in abundance from the building site. Arvid lived of Findus *barnmat*[100] in sterile jars. We never stayed in the *stuga* overnight in the beginning, as there was no furniture, toilet, or heating. The place smelled intensively of new paint.

One day the electrician managed to cut through the main cable under the roof and left in a hurry without telling us what to do.

We had to find and repair the fault ourselves. The plumber was no better. When he tried to screw the toilet to the floor, he drew the screw too tight, and the porcelain cracked. He also left in a hurry, and he never came back again.

There was a nasty accident only once. I was painting the kitchen and Walter was hacking all the roots away in front of the living room windows, clearing a path around the house. Suddenly I heard a scream and Walter came in holding Arvid whose face was covered in blood. Arvid had been curious as to what the chopping noises were. Standing close behind Walter he was an easy target when the axe was lifted again and came into contact with his forehead. We rushed to Nacka Hospital, my fingers full of paint and blood, Walter full of earth and blood. A sight for sore eyes. When Walter explained the accident: 'I hit my son with an axe', there was a sudden silence of mistrust but after explaining that we were working on our new house everyone relaxed, Arvid was stitched up, and we were sent home, rather pale.

8. Second child and further medical experiences

We realised that to be an only child with all attention being focused on one, is a lonely business. I was more than happy when I found out 1966 that I was pregnant again. Shortly afterwards, all three of us went off to Rhodes, knowing that we probably would not be able to afford another holiday for some time to come.

The pregnancy went well, no morning sickness, no dizzy spells, no craving for strange food. Once again, I put on very little weight and everything seemed fine. In the sixties, one had no chance to examine the embryo by ultra wave. Finally on 3 October 1966, we drove to Södersjukhuset,[101] as the birth pains came regularly. It was an easy birth and only took two and a half hours. Alexandra was a heavy weight of 2,880 g, length 51 cm, born at 2 o'clock at night.

The nurses took a long time before they showed us the baby, so we knew instinctively that there was a problem. We were concerned when we saw Alexandra's gum cleavage. We felt so helpless. The nurses were marvellous and helped us through the first days. They knew that this tiny tot could not breast feed as she had no sucking reflexes or, better said, could not suck even if she wanted to. However, she had to have breast milk, it being the best nourishment as well as building up her immunity system. Because part of the upper lip was missing, she caught every infection under the sun. I fed her with a special little cup, a spoonful at a time, slowly, slowly but surely. The procedure was repeated every four hours around the clock to keep Alexandra from starving.

Due to her many infections her first operation, which closed her upper lip, had to be postponed time and time again, eight times all in all. In the end, we both moved into the Sachsska Children's Hospital where she was kept in a sterile room. Of all 'bad timing', Arvid came down with scarlet fewer and was taken to the epidemic hospital. Nowadays the patients are given penicillin and after two weeks they are on their feet. However, we had to smoke out the flat etc. We were only allowed to visit him with a glass wall between us. He was so sad to be abandoned once again that he even refused to look at us.

Finally, Alexandra's blood count was down to normal, and Dr Grenabo, head of the department of plastic surgery at Sabbatsberg,[102] closed the cleavage and extended part of the lip. For years he had experimented for ways to make the four major operations for his little patients as successful as possible. His intention was to make his patients both nice looking and without any speech impediments. He was highly successful in his efforts and was considered the best in his field.

During Alexandra's first year we led a strange sort of life. She had to be kept away from crowds and avoid any place where she might catch an infection. No underground trains, no guests at home etc. Of course, we were outdoors a lot and lngarö was the perfect place for her during the summer. Arvid never commented on the comings and goings of his sister. Once when Walter was at home, Arvid made him aware of 'Deine Tochter, die da drinnen liegt und schreit'.[103] Arvid thought his new playmate was simply a nuisance.

After the second operation, at the age of two years, a new roof was stretched across Alexandra's upper gum valve. This was probably the most difficult and important operation in the whole series and life became much easier. Until now she had only been able to drink fluids and she could not talk. Now, suddenly, she could eat all sorts of food for her age, and she bubbled over with enthusiasm at all the wonderful sounds she could produce. She was such a cheerful child and as soon as we appeared in the hospital on our dozens of visits she was passed around by the staff as an old friend.

When she was three years old, we managed to get her into the Kindergarten at St. Eriks for a few hours each morning. It was vital that she could meet other children and she enjoyed these hours tremendously. Also, she learned to speak Swedish rather fast. She was a good organiser already at that age. Instead of hanging up her

Fig. 14. Lucie with daughter Alexandra, 1969 (courtesy of Alexandra Widl).

own coat she taught all the children that her peg had a strawberry symbol, in case they found some of her clothes lying around.

When Alexandra was about five years old, I began to notice that her hearing was deteriorating rather badly. Not strange, considering the many colds and ear-infections she had had. Despite assurances from a doctor that 'she will grow out of it', I knew I had to do more than just wait and see. At the back of my mind, I remembered Dr Grenabo telling me on our first visit 'if ever she has ear problems, remember we have an expert for these patients here'. As I forgot the expert's name, I knocked on many doors at Sabbatsberg until I finally managed to find out his name: Dr Lindahl. On many occasions he inserted tiny tubes in Alexandra's ears, giving remedy to her pains and healing her ear infections.

The last operations helped to shape her nose. On one occasion in Sabbatsberg she was not happy with the food provided by the hospital. On her own walking through endless cellar corridors, she managed to find the central kitchen and arranged her future

Fig. 15. Lucie and Walter Widl, c. 2010, which might be the time when this memoir was written (courtesy of Alexandra Widl).

menus – what a girl! A final nose correction was made about 1983, and to our relief the worst problems were over.

Appendix 1:
Kindertransport list
(Archive of the Jewish Community of Vienna, IKG)

- 6 -   2.2.39.

TRANSPORT OF CHILDREN FROM VIENNA			INTER-AID.
0112	Vienna II Schreigasse 19/18.	24.10.27.	
0113	Vienna X Favoritenstrasse 130.	2.7.22.	Emil.
0114	Vienna Vi Liniengasse 45	2.4.35.	Josef
0115	Vienna II Rueppgasse 9/7	29.5.21.	Abraham.
116	Vienna I Elizabethstrasse 5.		
117	Vienna II Zirkusgasse 27	1928	
118 119	"	1924	
Hans	Vienna VIII Piaristengasse 54	1928	
120	Vienna XVIII Haisingergasse 37	1923	
121 Hilsenrad Lucy	Vienna V Siebenbrunngasse 65	1930	
122 Hilsenrad Margit	"	1927	
123	Vienna VII Lindengasse 26	1924	
124	Vienna III Scarottgasse 11	1921	
125	Vienna III "	1926	
126	Vienna VII c/o Kellen Zieglergasse 20	1923	
127	Vienna XVIII Wiesaskstrasse 39.	1924.	
128	Vienna II Untere Donaustrasse 49	1923	
129	Vienna XIII Fichtnergasse 4.	1925.	
130	"	1922.	
131	Vienna VIII Kupagasse 6.	1923.	
132	Vienna IX Porzellangasse 55	1933	
133	Vienna II Karmnaustrasse 30/16	1921.	
134			

Case file Lucie Hilsenrad
World Jewish Relief (formerly Central British Fund)
Archives.

No. 4350

No. of H.O. Permit 2315   NAME HILSENRAD.   Luzie

Date of Birth 2. 1. 30   Religion J   Name and address of Parents
HILSENRAD   Ludwig Maria
65 Siebenbrunnengasse
Vienna 5

Date of arrival in England   Camp

Date left Camp   (1) Mrs Morrison, 62 Sherbrooke Ave, Glasgow.

English addresses   (2) "   "   8 Seafield Road, Ayr.

(3) Episcopal House, Castle Douglas.
Jo Aneill, 12 Falkland mansions, Hyndland, Glasgow, W.2.
Jan. 44, Pelton House Farm School, W.A.S.S. W A.S.E, Midlothian

Weekly amount (if any) paid to foster parents:

Responsible Area Committee: Glasgow Jewish Refugees Cttee.

N. Dec. 46: 92, Cazenove Rd., N.16

Guarantor: Mrs Morrison, 8 Seafield Road, Ayr.

Health: Good 24. 4. 40

Education: Primary School.

Re-emigration: None.

Welfare Rpt: Apr. 1943

2/11/39. To Mrs Brink from Miss Ellis, saying Mr & Mrs Morrison & his wife were still retaining Lucie & Margit

8/11/39. To Mr Ellis from after Carlisle. Reply to letter of Nov. 2nd

18/5/39. To Mrs Tuttman, suggesting he should look after Lucie & Margit for a short holiday period

31/5/39. Reply from Mrs Tuttman, saying no space accommodation in flat for Lucie & Margit

1st June 1939. To Mrs Tuttman see from Mr Morrison pointing out his obligations to his relations

23/May 1940. To Mrs Braidell from Mrs Ellis, asking the movement to reply direct to Mr Morrison, re his responsibility to bring out Lucie & Margit at his own expense.

21/10/42. From Glasgow Cttee - To Miss Jackson Reg. H enclosing welfare Reports on Lucie & Margit

2/10/42. To Miss Lauric from Bloomsbury House, requesting welfare reports on Lucie & Margit

24/10/42. From Miss Lauric to Miss Rig, enclosing the requested welfare reports

23/10/42 To Miss Lauric from Miss Rig, asking where the children Lucie & Margit were living

19/10/42 From Episcopal House saying Margit Hilsenrad was at school in Kirkcudbright.

14/10/42. From Head master Kirkcudbright saying Lucie was now in the First year of double language secondary course in Kirkcudbright

8/11/42. High School; Reg. Jackson. From Miss Rig to Miss Jackson acknowledging reports the same on welfare

20/Aug/43.   A copy of a letter from Miss C. D. Sloan to Sec. Glas. Cttee saying Mrs Morrison wished to discontinue payment in respect of Lucie & Margit Hirschmann.

3/Sept/43   From Miss Laurie to Miss C. D. Sloan, saying that re a copy of her letter received from Glas. Cttee; Miss Laurie would take up the matter with the Movement in London

3/Sept/43   To Miss L Lehmann from Reg.11. saying Miss Laurie would discuss matter of Mrs Morrison & the Hirschman children at the London meeting

6/Sept/43.   To Miss Laurie from Miss Lehmann acknowledging her letter date of 3rd.

10/9/43.   From Dr Burgner to Miss Laurie enclosing copy of Guarantee form

22/9/1943.   To Mrs Morrison from Miss Laurie, stating her cttee was responsible for upkeep of Lucie & Margit during their stay in this country

Excerpt from Letter from Bloomsbury House dated 24 Sept. 1943, asking what had been decided re Hirschman children.

24/9/1943.   From Mrs J. Morrison re maintenance of Hirschman children — to Miss Laurie in answer to letter of 22nd.

2/10/1943.   To Mr Hanson from Miss Laurie, enclosing copy of reply received from Mrs Jack Morrison

2/10/1943   To Mrs N Laski, from Miss Laurie Reg. 11, enclosing copy of correspondence with Mrs J. Morrison

13/10/1943.   To Mrs Morrison from Mrs Hardisty, re his decision to discontinue
(a copy of letter   payments for Lucie & Margit

14/10/1943   To Miss Laurie from Mrs J. Hanson, asking if she has any further information from 'Movement' re Margit & Lucie

14/10/43   To Region 11, from Glasgow Cttee enclosing communication received in relation to Lucie

15/10/43.   To Mrs Morrison from Miss Laurie Reg. 1, returning forms sent by her re 'Health Department' in letter of 14th oct.

15/11/43.   To Mrs Hanson from Reg.11. enclosing a copy of a letter sent to Mrs Morrison by the Movement — asking for welfare report on Margit.

20/10/43.   To Miss Laurie from Miss Lehmann, acknowledging a copy of Mrs Hardisty's letter to Mrs Morrison

18/10/43.   From Mrs J. Morrison to Mrs Hardisty, suggesting the 'Movement' is liable
a copy of a   responsibility of Hirschman children, also enclosing correspondence
letter   received from 'Health Department', to be dealt with

5/11/43.   From Mrs H. Burgner to Miss Laurie Reg. 11, enclosing copy of Mrs Morrison's letter of 5th oct. asking who was paying for the Hirschman girls' maintenance

12/11/43.   From Miss Laurie to Dr H. Burgner, saying still awaiting definite report from Glasgow re Lucie

13/11/43.   To Miss Lehmann from Miss Laurie, requesting welfare reports & information about Lucie & Margit

10/11/43.   To Miss Laurie from L. Lehmann, enclosing Head master & welfare report of Margit and Lucie, as requested

4350 HILSENRAD

Bn: 2.1.30 Lucie

J

(2)

19.12.46. Memo to Mrs.Hardisty re Lucie's training, fares, etc.

6.1.47. Sent B.71 to Mr. Micklewright.

20.3.47. To Mr.Morrison enclosing our acc. for Lucie's dressmaking
fees and maintenance at Cazenove Road.

32.3.47 HF/MM To girl asking her to get in touch with her guarantor
29. 4. 47.
PK/41. To Miss Laurie asking if she will explain the position re
Lucie being moved to London without consulting him first.
Enclosing copy of his letter to Mrs. Hardisty, and account
which he refused to pay.

15.4.47. To Mr. Morrison stating Lucie's need for a corset and pair
of shoes.

19.5.47 Permission from Mr Morrison to buy clothing.
21.5.47 Letter to Mrs Margulies re buying shoes, and corsets. HF/MM

3.6.47 Ltr. to Mr.Morrison enclosing account.

JHB/PC

15. 7. 47. Account for £51. 3. 11d. sent to Mr. Morrison.
PK/84.

3. 8. 47. To Morrison, asking to settle account.outstanding.
PK/84

15.8.47 Ltr.fr.Mr.Morrison re maintenance. Letter discussed with
HF/MM Mrs.Hardisty.Decided to discuss matter with Lucy.
21.8.47 Ltr.to Lucy asking her to make an appt.to see Miss Feldman

29.8.47 HF/MM Further ltr.to Lucy asking her to contact Miss Feldman

3.9.47 HF/MM Lucie called. Had been away for a fortnight on holiday at
a Kibbutz in Bedford. Informed me that she had seen her
guarantor Mr.Morris who had told her in effect what he had
written to Mrs.Hardisty regarding future employment etc.
Lucy is to leave school and is to discuss with her Head
Master the possibility of employment in the immediate
future. Told her that if he was unable to find her a satisfac-
tory situation we cd. easily place her through Miss Abrahams
of the J.B.G. Lucy has promised to contact us again after
she has discussed the matter with her Head Master.

4.9.47 HF/MM Lucy called and informed me that she had found
employment with "Suzanne" Costierre,36 Beauchamp Pl.S.W.3
is to commence on Monday Sept.8th on a months trial.
Starting wage £5.10.0 p.w.

4.9.47 Note to Mrs.Hardisty and to accounts that parents are
living in Vienna.

7.10.47. Letter to Mr. Morrison informing him that Lucie has taken up
employment with a good class dressmaker, and asking him to
settle the account for 251.3.11d.

- 4 -

21.10.47. To Mr. Morrison ack. cheque.

12.12.47 Ltr.fr.Lucy enquiring about possibility of visiting
parents in Vienna. Note sent to Mrs.Braun

24.12.47 Girl called sent her to Mrs Braun, Over Seas Dept., to deal
with Austrian passport etc.

2.1.1.48 To girl enclosing T.D.form for Travel Document.

27.1.48 KB To girl:Must apply for Austrian passport and visa.When
granted get re-entry permit. Visits to Austria allowed on
compassionate grounds only.

24.2.48. Report on Wards made out. HF/Si.

17.3.48 Visited Cazenove Rd.hostel.Informed by Mrs Margulies that
JS/MM Lucy is desperately wanting to visit her parents in Vienna,
especially as the Father is in poor health.Told Mrs.
Margulies that Lucy can get a doctor's certificate confirm-
ing the Father's condition. She co.no doubt then be able to visit
Vienna on compassionate grounds. Mrs.Margulies says that
Lucy has grown into an extremely capable and well mannered
young girl. She is an asset to the hostel.

13.4.48 *Memo to Mrs Margulies re funds for visit to
Vienna — D Certificates confirming fathers
illness attached.*

27.4.48. Letter to Mr. Margulies per registered post enclosing two
medical certificates which Lucie will need when she goes
to the Austrian Consulate for her visa to visit her parents
in Vienna.

5.5.48. To girl - Movement will pay girl's fare to Austria but we
would like to know exact amount. HF/JS.

13.5.48 Lucie called for cheque . Is leaving for Vienna on 19.5.48
is most grateful to Movement for making this visit to see
parents possible.

A 22701

Case No.

H.O. Ref. 2315

JEWISH REFUGEES COMMITTEE

4310

Surname: HILSENRAD

Other Names: LUZIE

Address

Phone No.

Date of Birth: 7.1.1930   Nationality: Austrian   Born at: VIENNA   If Orthodox

Address in Germany: VIENNA   Date of arrival in England: 12.1.1939   PERMIT Valid for

Married   Husband / Wife   Not in England   Number of Children: Born at / Age / Sex / If in Eng.

Relatives or Friends in England, Stating Financial Position

Means: In England / Germany / Elsewhere   Amount   Country S/6/49   b.

OCCUPATION in Germany (in full detail)

Alternative Occupations   Experience

Languages

If registered by any other Refugee Committee   Passport Expires

LEFT ENGLAND FOR   ON

Date of Interviews   Port of Arrival   Nature of Hospitality / Means Grant / Initials

Transferred to I.R.C. 30/6/1948   LY

21.04, visited [...] at [...]. Is a well mannered pleasant respectful young person making good progress in her trade. Has good news from parents in Vienna, though father still in very poor health.   HF.

21.2.48 [...]

3.1.48 [...]

P.T.O

Date of Interview	Port of Arrival		Nature of Hospitality	Money Grant	Initials

11.5.49 Lttr. to Lucy re registration as British citizen. Hope she has the £10

13.5.49 Lucy called asks if we can lend her £5.0.0. for Registration fee — she had saved some money, but recently bought some clothes. The girl has been self-supporting for a little while — only earns just over £4.0.0 per week — will repay loan in weekly instalments.

16.5.49 Agree to loan of £5.—— (free) Ex.C.

16.5.49 Lttr. to Lucie infmg. her that Mrs. Roon agrees to loan and asking her to call on Wednesday lunch time

18.5.49 Lucy called, signed Loan Agreement for £5.

19.5.49 Lttr. to Lucy enclosing £5. loan twds. Nat. fee

1.6.49 British by naturalization.

13.6.49 Lttr. to R. Levine for consent for Lucie to hold British P/port.

13.6.49 Lucie called — repaid £3.0.0 of the £5.0.0 loaned to her — would like to visit her parents in Austria again this summer — will owe money to pay her own fare after she has repaid loan to us. Conscientious young woman — gives very good impression.

15.6.49 Note to R. Palmer re ......

16.6.49 consent to hold British P/port signed by Mr. Levine

20.7.49 Lucie called. repaid £2.0.0. has now discharged her debt to the JRC. Is saving for fare to Vienna — may stay there for 2 or 3 months to take Cutting & Designing Course.

3.8.49 No action required from our angle.

10.8.49 Lucie called — Is leaving this country for Austria next week. needed Nut case — gave voucher for one.

17.8.49 Had received phone saying had been led for more expense than originally anticipated in arranging her journey to Vienna — Girl was leaving this country tomorrow & literally no money to see her through her journey — therefore arranged to give her £7. which I would refund from our ..... special account

JEWISH REFUGEES COMMITTEE

Case No.

H.O. Ref.

Surname

Other Names Lucie

Address

Phone No.

Date of Birth

Nationality

Born at

If Orthodox

Address in Germany

Date of arrival in England

PERMIT Valid for

Married

Husband / Wife Not in England

Number of Children
Born at	Age	Sex	If in Eng.

Relatives or Friends in England (Stating Financial Position)

Means	in England	Amount	Country
	Germany		
	Elsewhere		

OCCUPATION in Germany (in full detail)

Alternative Occupations

Experience

Languages

If registered by any other Refugee Committee

Passport Expires

LEFT ENGLAND FOR　　　　　ON

Date of Interviews	Port of Arrival	Nature of Hospitality	Money Grant	Initials

18.7.49 Letter to Mrs. Margulies enclosing 10/- which Mrs.M. had advanced to Lucie for her journey to ——

23.9.50 Lucy still in Vienna with parents. For —— of Guardianship.

—— Undertaking —— notifies that —— was born on ——, but is still living in Vienna.　　RF/G

18/7/50 See letter from L dated 6/7/50, stating that she will
probably remain in Vienna until early next year—
will be 21 in January.
Checked with Mr. Margulies and understand that all the
girls who left at the Hostel are now booked (about 10)
and can remain here for the time being　　　RF/G

Date of Interviews	Port of Arrival			Nature of Hospitality	Money Grant	Initials
	A.77701 SILBERRAD Lucie 7.1.30	Zielas Pfarrg. 1/6, Vienna II	Naturalised. Went to visit aunts in Vienna last September. Plans to return to U.S. early next year. Has enough correspondence.			

Extracts from memoir books
by Bengt Rösiö
(in original Swedish language)

Bengt Rösiö, *Yrke: Diplomat* (Stockholm: Norstedt, 1988).

'Jag följde sommarkursen på Haagakademin för internationell rätt men hade aptit på nästan allting utom internationell rätt. Därifrån reste jag till Wien och blev inskriven vid universitetet för höstterminen 1949. [...] På en studentutflykt i Grinzing träffade jag en ung judinna, Lucinda, och sedan var det mest hon och jag. Vi gick på teatern, tredje radens sida, ibland på bio, ibland på operan, på museer när det var gratisdagar. Efteråt satt vi på något kafe och beställde varsin The [sic!] mit Zitrone och ingen opponerade sig mot den billiga förtäringen – nästan alla wienare var fattiga och Wien en trött och härjad stad. Jag följde henne till fots hem till Leopoldstadt, den judiska stadsdelen som låg i det sovjetryska distriktet; hennes föräldrar levde alltjämt ehuru man gått illa åt hennes pappa. Lucinda hade man i tid fått ut till London.' (28)

'Våren 1950 låg jag vid Sorbonne. Lucinda kom dit och jag hade skrivit ihop tillräckligt med artiklar för att vi skulle [28] kunna åka till Marocko. Vi tog en buss från Casablanca till Marrakech och sedan över Atlasbergen in i öknen – detta var ju många år innan turismen kom igång. Från Tanger tog vi båten över till Algeciras, och jag minns mosaikplattorna på torget i Granada och rosorna i Sevilla. Ibland var det svårt med vägglössen men de bekom oss inte så mycket, och vi tog oss vidare till Portugal och så småningom till Toledo och El Greco. Till slut nådde jag målet Andorra [...] Andorra la Vella var då alltjämt bara en vanlig katalansk by, inte en turist så långt ögat kunde nå. [...] Från lumpen återvände jag till Paris för att vara praktikant på svenska handelskammaren. Lucinda kom dit och följde sedan också med till Sverige där hon fick arbete som modist.' (29)

'På sommaren [1952] gjorde jag och Lucinda en resa ner till Dalmatien. Vi tog tåg över Zagreb, och från Split åkte vi båt till Dubrovnik. Där fanns inte en turist vid den tiden, och det begynnande femtiotalets Dubrovnik – Ragusa, som Lucindas far kallade det – tillhörde alltjämt dalmatierna. Vi älskade staden och en kväll såg vi Hamlet spelas på serbokroatiska på stadsmurens krön. Vi tog bussen från Kotor upp till Montenegro på den gamla grusvägen, vandrade i Cetinje och tog sedan tåget tillbaka över Mostar och Sarajevo.' (33)

'Jag låg i vaccinationsfeber och läste Artur Lundkvists India-brand – jag hade en månad på mig innan jag skulle resa. Kort dessförinnan hade Koestler gett ut sin självbiografi, Arrow in the blue. Han berättade hur han en kväll kom på bron över Donau Kanal – samma som jag brukade gå hem på från Leopoldstadt – och plötsligt fick ingivelsen att slänga sina medicinska läroböcker i vattnet och bryta upp. Jag begrep att jag måste göra detsamma med Lucinda, kände att det var ett nytt skede som trängde sig på mig. Hon följde mig till Bromma [flygfält] men vi visste båda att vi höll på att glida isär.' (34)

Bengt Rösiö, *Hermelin bland katter: Ett rapsodiskt och ganska kalejdoskopiskt collage av anteckningar, rapporter, artiklar, brev och annan skrivklåda i och utanför UD-tjänst 1947–2007* (Täby: privat tryck, 2009).

'Man har så konstiga minnen [...] Jag minns en dag 1950 i en marockansk by när jag satt på taket till ett vandrarhem tillsammans med Lucinda, den unga judinna jag reste med. En marockansk städerska gick runt och flyttade damm, hade en unge med sig. Lucinda gjorde en liten snurra av papper och gav barnet, pengar hade vi just inga att ge. Det dröjde ett tag innan flickan begrep hur det hela var tänkt men så hajade hon och hennes ansikte lyste upp, första gången hon fick en leksak.' (8)

'En familj jag känner bor i det krigshärjade Leopoldstadt och de är de enda i huset som har rinnande vatten.' (19)

'Ur ett brev till min farbror Hilding 26 maj 1982
Försommaren 1950 kom jag dit [Portugal]. Jag åkte med en flicka, en österrikisk judinna med vilken jag fann mycket gemensamt och mycket olikt. Det var så med många jag kände på den tiden - de längtade efter trygghet, jag ville bort från den. Vi fann varandra i detta sökande mot skilda mål, en gemenskap i tryggheten lika väl som i flykten.

Vi lämnade Sevilla med tåg och kom i kvällningen fram till gränsfloden, Guadiana. Vi tog färjan över och strövade på gatorna i en stad som hette San Antonio nånting, såg de vita husen och de blå azulejosmotiven för första gången. Solen sjönk och färgerna övergick i purpur och milda nyanser av violett, och vi måste väl ha ätit nånstans fast vi sällan hade råd att dricka vin.

Vi tog ett nattåg till Lissabon, tredje klass eftersom det inte fanns fjärde. Att sova sittande i en fullsatt kupe var inget problem och på morgonen kom vi fram till Tejo och ännu efter mer än trettio år minns jag lystern över floden, Lissabons skönhet, bullret och stånkandet från färjan, människorna, livet, ljuset, allt detta som var så fjärran den grå tristess i Sverige där man lever i ett säreget skymningsljus där alla katter är grå och de som verkligen är grå trivs bäst. Vi tog på oss ryggsäckarna och gick i land, sökande efter ett hotell som var billigt nog och sen gick vi ut på stan och upptäckte Alfama.

Vi åkte ut till Sintra och smyglyssnade till en guide som talade för amerikanska turister, däribland en kvinna som sa att "Om Ni kunde sälja det här till Amerika skulle Ni få bra betalt." Det var under åren kring och efter Marshallhjälpen. Vi låg över natten i en stad som hette Caldas da Rainha och åkte vidare till Nazare som då var ett sömnigt fiskeläge. Vi bodde i en liten pension och strövade på den tomma stranden, bland uppdragna fiskebåtar med vackra mönster, badade i havet och åt fisk. Sen Coimbra med sitt gamla universitet där vi satt och pratade med portugisiska studenter. Oporto med sina husfasader fyllda med tvätt upphängd på streck mellan piskbalkongerna. Ett smutsigt nattåg som stannade på varenda station tog oss fram till gränsen och sen till Salamanca där vi måste leta länge efter rum eftersom det var fotbollsmatch i staden. Det måste ha varit på resan därifrån till Madrid som vi såg Escorial – herregud, vi visste inte ens att det fanns. Sen Toledo och El Greco.' (20)

'Sen sökte jag ett UD-stipendium och fick 3.000. Haagakademin först, sen Wien. Och Wien 1948 var Den tredje mannens värld där Harry Limes steg smög i gränderna mellan tunga barockpalats och Anton Karas cittra klang i skymningen. The [sic!] mit Zitrone på Cafe Mozart efter Operan eller Theater in der Josefstadt, tredje radens sida, med Lucinda, den judinna jag senare förlovade mig med. Spårvagn ut till Grinzing, ett spräckligt studentliv och mötet med en stad i ruiner, värst i Leopoldstadt där Lucindas familj bodde. Jag gick alltid hem därifrån på den lilla bron över Donau Kanal, den från vilken Arthur Koestler slängde sina böcker när han plötsligt beslöt bryta upp.

Det var med Lucinda jag åkte till Portugal. Dessförinnan hade vi rest i Marocko, bott på vandrarhem i Marrakech och vägglössiga serajer ute i öknen. Sen till Spanien och Portugal som jag berättade om i brevet till min farbror Hilding [...] Det var nånstans i Spanien som vi skulle försöka komma med ett nattåg. En tandlös gammal bärare erbjöd sig fixa sittplats men vi hade inte råd att betala honom och den rappa Lucinda lyckades hugga två platser när vi trängde oss in [21] med våra ryggsäckar och medpassagerarna tveksamt betraktade oss och frågade Matrimonio [Gifta]? På ett spår intill stod ett nattåg till Madrid, med wagonslits och rika människor. Själv var jag nöjd på min träbänk men undrade hur det skulle kännas att åka sovvagn.' (22)

Endnotes

Introduction (p. 7–10)

[1] Jennifer Craig-Norton, *The Kindertransport: Contesting Memory* (Bloomington: Indiana University Press, 2019); Andrea Hammel, *The Kindertransport: What Really Happened* (Cambridge: Polity, 2024).

[2] Frances Williams, *The Forgotten Kindertransportees: The Scottish Experience* (London: Bloomsbury, 2014).

[3] Most of the survivors were living in mixed marriages. See Herbert Exenberger, Johann Koss, and Brigitte Ungar-Klein, *Kündigungsgrund Nichtarier: Die Vertreibung Jüdischer Mieter aus den Wiener Gemeindebauten in den Jahren 1938–1939* (Wien: Picus, 1996), p. 81.

[4] 'Geburts-Anzeige', Matrikel-Amt, Archives of the Jewish Community of Vienna.

[5] Norbert Götz, *Ungleiche Geschwister: Die Konstruktion von nationalsozialistischer Volksgemeinschaft und schwedischem Volksheim* (Nomos, Baden-Baden, 2001), 72, 129, 295, 319, 392, 400–402, 530f.

[6] Vera K. Fast, *Children's Exodus: A History of the Kindertransport* (London: I.B. Tauris, 2011), p. 124.

1. Childhood in Austria (p. 13–17)

[1] Lucie's mother, Maria Hilsenrad (1893–1981), born Maria Krchák in Vienna. She left the Catholic church and was thereafter recorded as non-affiliated.

[2] Lucie's father, Ludwig Hilsenrad (1884–1968), born in Suceava, Bukovina, in the Austrian Empire, today Romania. In 1908 he emigrated to Vienna. He participated in the First World War 1915–1918 with deployment in Herzegovina and in 1920 became an Austrian citizen. Vienna directories list him as a pharmacy employee or pharmacist, M.A. See *Wiener Adreßbuch: Lehmanns Wohnungsanzeiger* 73, no. 1 (1932), p. 589; *Wiener Adreßbuch: Lehmanns Wohnungsanzeiger* 79, no. 1 (1938), p. 452. We do not know what led to his emigration but

as a Jew from East Central Europe, Ludwig Hilsenrad belonged to a group of immigrants who are generally said to have come to Vienna primarily to escape persecution and economic strife, while also being attracted by the metropolitan opportunities of the capital. See Ilana Fritz Offenberger, *The Jews of Nazi Vienna, 1938–1945: Rescue and Destruction* (Cham: Springer, 2017), p. 11.

[3] They married in 1925.

[4] Margit Hilsenrad (1927–2019). See also notes 32 and 56.

[5] This refers to the Graben-Apotheke 'Zum schwarzen Bären', one of the oldest pharmacies in Vienna, located at Graben 7, adjacent to Stephansplatz.

[6] According to his official property declaration of 1938, Ludwig Hilsenrad's assets were limited to his RM 43,472 pension accruals. In addition, he declared a golden watch and a wedding ring, together worth RM 100 (Austrian State Archives, Archiv der Republik, Vermögensverkehrstelle, File 39185). The property declaration was requested by a decree concerning the Reporting of Jewish Assets (*Vermögensanmeldung*) of 26 April 1938, requiring Jewish citizens to report their domestic and foreign assets if the total value exceeded 5,000 RM. Three weeks later, an agency was created to oversee the transfer of such Jewish assets into Aryan hands (*Vermögensverkehrstelle*).

[7] Unclear what this might refer to.

[8] The Austrian province of Carinthia.

[9] A brief account of the destruction of Willi Pollak's photography business by the Nazis is provided in the English language article by Walter Mentzel, 'Willi Pollak', in *Lexicon of Austrian Provenance Research* (Vienna: Commission for Provenance Research, 2019), available at https://www.lexikon-provenienzforschung.org/en/pollak-wilhelm, accessed 1 November 2024.

[10] The school and character reports are no longer available.

[11] The German Reich incorporated Austria on 12 March 1938, extending the Nazi terror to this German speaking country with which it was historically affiliated. Throughout most of the 1930s, Ludwig Hilsenrad was listed in the public address book *Wiener Adreßbuch: Lehmanns Wohnungsanzeiger*, but he no longer appeared after 1938. According to registry data of the city of Vienna, the Hilsenrads moved

six times between 1938 and 1945, but the official data may fail to give the full picture, especially as any contact with authorities involved considerable risk for people of Jewish background. From 1925 until May 1936, the Hilsenrads lived in an apartment in Alberichgasse 2 in the XVth district. They then moved to an apartment at Akazienhof 12 in the XIIth district (Meidling), probably because they needed more space for their daughters. This apartment (which the memoir mentions they were forced to leave) was part of the now heritage-protected George-Washington-Hof housing estate, a product of the progressive Viennese housing policy at the time. A general background on the expulsion of Jews from communal housing is given by Herbert Exenberger, Johann Koss, and Brigitte Ungar-Klein in *Kündigungsgrund Nichtarier: Die Vertreibung Jüdischer Mieter aus den Wiener Gemeindebauten in den Jahren 1938–1939* (Wien: Picus, 1996). Following this, from August 1938 to November 1940, Ludwig Hilsenrad and Maria Hilsenrad were registered separately, but at the same address, Siebenbrunnegasse 65 in the Vth district. Throughout the rest of the war, the couple was registered together at various addresses. Their last three appartments were in the neighbourhood of Leopoldstadt, the primarily Jewish district of Vienna where the Nazis concentrated the Jewish population. After the war, the Hilsenrads remained in this area, living at Kleine Pfarrgasse 3 from 1947 until the death of Ludwig Hilsenrad in 1968 (Municipal and Provincial Archives of Vienna, Registration Records).

[12] The first eight weeks after the Nazi takeover of Austria were characterised by an initial wave of public and private harassment of the Jews, the so-called Anschluss Pogrom. See Offenberger, *Jews of Nazi Vienna*, pp. 31–67.

[13] Derived from the euphemistic German word *(Reichs-)Kristallnacht*. The English term is Night of Broken Glass or November pogrom, a poltically organised progrom on 9/10 November 1938 that vandalised Jewish institutions, businesses, and properties nationwide.

[14] Rosa Krchák (1873–1937), born in Schildberg (Štíty), Czech lands.

[15] Anton Krchák (1862–1941), born in Göding (Hodonín), a town on the Czech side of the Czech–Slovakian border region.

[16] Noble house owner.

[17] After being indicted on 29 November 1939, Maria Hilsenrad was sentenced to eight months in prison on 8 March 1940 under §2(2) of

the Nazi Treachery Act of 1934 (*Gesetz gegen heimtückische Angriffe auf Staat und Partei und zum Schutz der Parteiuniformen*). The judgement was retroactively annulled after the war on 24 December 1949. See Municipal and Provincial Archives of Vienna, WStLA, Sondergericht, A1: SHv 9098/47. Maria Hilsenrad had been released from prison by 29 July 1940, after almost five months, and later received a total of 4,300 Austrian Schillings in reparations as a political victim of National Socialism through the 'Fonds der Sammelstelle B'. (For this and the indictment, see Austrian State Archives, Archiv der Republik, Sammelstelle II/A, Zl. 780, with reference to case Landgericht Wien, OA, W 10397.) Contrary to what Lucie Widl believed, Maria's incarceration occurred at the beginning of the Second World War. This timing might have saved Ludwig Hilsenrad's life because anti-Jewish policies within the Nazi realm intensified towards the war's end.

[18] For insight into forced labor during this period, see Wolf Gruner, *Zwangsarbeit und Verfolgung: Österreichische Juden im NS-Staat 1938–45* (Innsbruck: Studien-Verlag, 2000). Ludwig Hilsenrad, who had a monthly salary of RM 595 before losing his pharmacy job in 1938, faced a reduced income between RM 281 and RM 288 thereafter. In 1948, he received an official Austrian victim's certificate (*Opferausweis*). Subsequently, in the 1960s, he (and after his death, his widow Maria Hilsenrad) received a total of 22,800 Austrian Schillings in reparations as a Jewish survivor (Austrian State Archives, Archiv der Republik, Sammelstelle A, Zl. 3.012). This compensation was part of the Austrian Republic's restitution efforts for Jewish victims of National Socialism through the 'Fonds der Sammelstelle A', a fund pooling asset of victims of National Socialism who did not (or were unable to) raise any restitution claims. See Margot Werner and Michael Wladika, *Die Tätigkeit der Sammelstellen* (Vienna: Oldenbourg, 2004).

[19] The Nazis did not consider subtle differences such as mixed marriages or 'mixed offspring' in occupied territories in Eastern Europe. However, to avoid social unrest within the German Reich proper, mixed marriages there generally offered relative protection from deportation until the end of the war. This also applied to Austria, although Austria experienced a somewhat more aggressive policy compared to Germany. For further insight into the conditions in Vienna and Austria, see Evan Burr Bukey, *Jews and Intermarriage in Nazi Austria* (Cambridge: Cambridge University Press, 2011); Offenber-

ger, *Jews of Nazi Vienna*; Patricia Fritz, '"Mischehen" in der NS-Zeit: Eine Betrachtung der Lebensformen der im Raum Wien beheimateten Eheleute einer Jüdisch–Christlichen "Mischehe" mit Ausblick auf die Leben der daraus hervorgegangenen Kinder', MA thesis (Graz: Karl-Franzens-Universität, 2018), available at https://unipub.uni-graz.at/obvugrhs/download/pdf/2679667, accessed 1 November 2024.

2. Kindertransport experience (p. 19–23)

[20] The connection of the November progrom, school bans, and Kindertransport has been noted by Rebekka Göpfert, *Der Jüdische Kindertransport von Deutschland nach England 1938/39: Geschichte und Erinnerung* (Frankfurt/Main: Campus, 1999), pp. 36–37. See also Renate Göllner, *Schule und Verbrechen: Die Vertreibung Jüdischer Schülerinnen und Schüler von Wiens Mittelschulen* (Frankfurt/Main: Lang, 2009).

[21] Documents in the Archive of the Jewish Community of Vienna (IKG) show that Lucie and Margit Hilsenrad were part of a child evacuation transport (*Kindertransport*) from Vienna to England that departed 10 January 1939 (see Appendix I). Their evacuation was facilitated by the Movement for the Care of Children from Germany (British Inter-Aid Committee), which was later renamed Refugee Children's Movement (RCM). At the time, Lucie was in fact nine years old and Margit eleven-and-a-half.

[22] The exact timing of Lucie's arrival in Scotland remains unclear. However, records show that she reached the port of Harwich in England on 12 January 1939. See Case file Lucie Hilsenrad, World Jewish Relief (formerly Central British Fund) Archives.

[23] For background on the Kindertransport scheme from Vienna, see Paul Weindling, 'The Kindertransport from Vienna: The Children Who Came and Those Left Behind', *Jewish Historical Studies* 51 (2019); Anna Wexberg-Kubesch, *Vergiss nie, dass Du ein jüdisches Kind bist: Der Kindertransport nach England 1938/39* (Wien: Mandelbaum, 2013).

[24] The following account, with its harsh valuations, reflects a young child's trauma of being driven away from home and separated from her parents, and the culture shock of finding herself in the position of a refugee. The British Refugee Children's Movement took efforts to place refugee minors in individual foster homes, rather than in

institutional children's homes. See Judith Tydor Baumel-Schwartz, *Never Look Back: The Jewish Refugee Children in Great Britain, 1938–1945* (West Lafayette, In: Purdue University Press, 2012), pp. 112, 127. However, this did not generally mitigate the emergence of such a double trauma because the notion of substantial integration with host families was lacking in the moral economy of the Kindertransport. Although efforts were generally made to keep siblings together, Lucie and Margit were fortunate, as this was far from always the case. The current memoir does not detail the process of how Lucie and Margit were paired with their host family. Families who had not sponsored a specific child were ordinarily invited by refugee committees to choose among the available children on the spot reminiscent of an animal market. Notably, the account given here contrasts starkly with children mentioned in the literature who came to affluent homes where these young refugees and their education are said to have abundantly been provided for. See Vera K. Fast, *Children's Exodus: A History of the Kindertransport* (London: I.B. Tauris, 2011), pp. 41, 43, 49. In general, the present account illustrates the conclusion of recent research that many pairings of refugee children and carers 'were far from happy' (Craig-Norton, *Kindertransport*, p. 319).

[25] This pertains to the family of Ann (1905–1980) and Jack Morrison (1902–1977), residing in Glasgow along with their children, Majorie and Michael. Ann Morrison, formerly De Jong, served as the 'guarantor' formally responsible for the Hilsenrad girls. Jack was the son of immigrants from Tallinn, Estonia, who had changed their surname from Myerson to Morrison a few years after settling in the UK. The Morrisons established a popular retail chain specialising in women's fashion. Within this family enterprise Jack Morrison held a leading role, overseeing real estate acquisitions. See Kappy Flanders and Andy Bronfman, *Sis & Pa: Our Family Album* (n.l.: author's edition, 2003). Jack is remembered as a leading philanthropist and was president of B'nai B'rith in Glasgow, a Jewish humanitarian charity, during the Second World War (and later grand president of the British and Irish B'nai B'rith). He was also active in numerous other Jewish civil society organisations, such as the Council for German Refugees, and was a member of the Talmud Torah board in Glasgow. On Morrison, see 'Obituary: Jack Morrison', *Jewish Chronicle*, 2 Sept. 1977. By contrast to Lucie's and Margit's experience, most of the foster families of Kindertransport children were actually Christian. See Andrea

Hammel, *The Kindertransport: What Really Happened* (Cambridge: Polity, 2024), p. 39.

[26] The British acceptance of the refugees was based on the idea of training the Kindertransport children for a future life in the colonies and Palestine. It was generally expected that the children would have entered some vocational training scheme by the age of sixteen, whereas their consideration of intellecttual or white-collar professions was discouraged. See Baumel-Schwartz, *Never Look Back*, p. 124.

[27] We do not know how Jack Morrison justified this decision to himself, but the theory of effective altruism would have urged him to save the lives of additional refugees, rather than expend his resources on the well-being of someone whom he already had saved. See Norbert Götz, Georgina Brewis, and Steffen Werther, *Humanitarianism in the Modern World: The Moral Economy of Famine Relief* (Cambridge: Cambridge University Press, 2020), p. 146.

[28] This brings Morrison's purchase of a Stradivarius violi, for which he paid the then record price of £22,000, in 1968, into the narrative. Morrison gave regular public performances as a violinist, and he was first violin with the Civil Service Orchestra of London ('Obituary: Jack Morrison', *Jewish Chronicle*, 2 Sept. 1977; see also 'Antonio Stradivari, Cremona, 1709, the "Marie Hall, Viotti"', available at https://tarisio.com/cozio-archive/property/?ID=41348, accessed 1 November 2024.

[29] The Morrison family had to cover the costs for 'boarding out' Lucie and Margit. Jack Morrison later discontinued payments and made efforts to be relieved from responsibility, but ultimately settled his debt. See Case file Lucie Hilsenrad, World Jewish Relief (formerly Central British Fund) Archives. Somewhat counterintuitively, research suggests that children residing in refugee homes tended to be happier than those staying with families. See Rebekka Göpfert, *Der jüdische Kindertransport von Deutschland nach England 1938/39: Geschichte und Erinnerung* (Frankfurt/Main: Campus, 1999), p. 126; Fast, *Children's Exodus*, p. 42.

[30] A sort of spooky, abandoned castle. The Skelmorlie Hostel was opend at the end of April 1940 by the Glasgow Jewish Education Board in collaboration with the Talmud Torah Council (*Jewish Chronicle*, 3 May 1940, p. 17). For images of the Skelmorlie 'castle' and excerpts from an oral history account, see 'The Birkenward' (available at

https://www.skelmorlievillas.co.uk/skelmorlie-villas/the-birkenward/, accessed 1 November 2024). According to information provided by the Scottish Jewish Archives Centre on the Birkenward Hostel, 'Between 1940 and 1943, around 60 refugee children and evacuees were housed in Birkenward, a large house in Skelmorlie, Ayrshire. It was described as: "a fully-equipped and adequately staffed Jewish Boarding School with full provisions within the premises for general and Jewish education, kosher meals and an ideal Jewish atmosphere…"' (available at https://www.ukholocaustmap.org.uk/map/records/birkenward-hostel, accessed 1 November 2024).

[31] This appears to have been long before Skelmorlie's actual closure at the beginning of 1943 (*Jewish Chronicle*, 12 February 1943, p. 10). Ernespie House was part of Castle Douglas in Dumfries and Galloway, which opened for refugee children in September 1940 (*Jewish Chronicle*, 6 September 1940, p. 12). For an image of some children living there in 1941, see 'Photo of evacuees' (available at https://sjac-collection.is.ed.ac.uk//record/111212, accessed 1 November 2024). The house was later converted into a hotel (see https://www.ernespiehouse.com/, accessed 1 November 2024).

[32] According to Margit's CV in the staff records of the World Health Organisation (WHO), she attended Kirkcudbright Academy, Kirkcudbright, Scotland, 1941–1944, graduating with a Senior Leaving Certificate. However, as mentioned in connection with a Chanukah celebration, Margit also seems to have spent some time at the Castle Douglas Hostel (i.e., Ernespie House; see *Jewish Echo*, 1 January 1941, p. 11). She appears to have been one of six girls relocated from Castle Douglas who were to be trained in various occupations in order to 'eventually be able to support themselves'. See *Jewish Chronicle*, 3 October 1941, p. 12.

[33] The Hebrew word (also transliterated as *hakhshara*) literally means 'preparation'. The term is connected to the Zionist Youth Aliyah movement and used for agricultural centres and training programmes such as that at Whittingehame House near Edinburg. According to the literature, participants came in groups with a Zionist background. See Göpfert, *Der jüdische Kindertransport*, pp. 123–127; Baumel-Schwartz, *Never Look Back*, pp. 137–152. By contrast, Lucie's and Margit's participation in the programme was arbitrary, as there is no indication of ideological commitment from their side. Nevertheless, they crossed the organisational line between the Refugee Child-

ren's Movement and the Youth Aliyah. Although the memoir describes Ernespie as different from Skelmorlie, it was run by the same Jewish Glasgow institutions. On issues of the two hostels, including overcrowding and financial problems, see *Jewish Chronicle*, 27 June 1941, p. 18, and 21 Nov. 1941, p. 16.

[34] As the hostel at Castle Douglas (Ernespie) was closed in December 1943 and the remaining evacuee children transferred to Glasgow and Edinburgh (*Jewish Chronicle*, 18 August 1944, p. 10), it remains unclear where the events described in the following paragraphs took place.

[35] Research has noted hostility between Kindertransport children and concentration camp survivors; see Fast, *Children's Exodus*, p. 155.

[36] Secondary school.

[37] Dressmaking was a common vocational training option offered to Kindertransport girls; see Baumel-Schwartz, *Never Look Back*, p. 125.

[38] Research has noted the disappointment among Kindertransportees when they found out that rudimentary education was often considered sufficient for them as refugee children (Hammel, *Kindertransport*, p. 87).

3. Post-war life in London (p. 25–27)

[39] Lucie lived from December 1946 to August 1949 in a hostel at Cazenove Rd. 16, in Hackney, north London, in an area that is today the heart of the Ultra-Orthodox Jewish community. Despite the clash of lifestyle, relief officers regarded Lucie at the time to have 'grown into an extremely capable and well mannered young girl', being 'an asset to the Hostel'. See, Case file Lucie Hilsenrad, World Jewish Relief (formerly Central British Fund) Archives.

[40] Margarethe Charoux, born Treibl (1895–1985), an international textile trader of Jewish background, and Siegfried Charoux, born Buchta (1896–1967), sculptor and left-wing political caricaturist; they emigrated in 1935 from Austria to England.

[41] Wilhelm Furtwängler (1886–1954), German conductor.

[42] This memoir refers to Margarethe Charoux by the name of Margit.

[43] David Astor (1912–2001) worked for *The Observer*, which was owned by his father at the time. He later became co-owner and long-time editor.

[44] Professor honoris causa, 1958, Akademie der bildenden Künste Wien / Academy of Fine Arts Vienna.

[45] The Charoux Museum, established in 1982, is today part of the Langenzersdorf Museum. For background, see Elisabeth Koller-Glück, 'Siegfried Charoux und das Charoux-Museum in Langenzersdorf', *Neues Museum*, no. 2 (1994).

[46] ORT is an acronym for *Obshestvo Remeslennogo i zemledelcheskogo Truda*, i.e., Society for Trades and Agricultural Labour. The organisation was founded in St Petersburg, Tsarist Russia, in 1880 to provide employable skills for Russia's impoverished Jews. A British branch opened in 1921, mainly engaging in fundraising for the World ORT Union's international projects. Post-war British ORT provided Jewish refugees and camp survivors with vocational training that ranged from nautical skills to dressmaking. The London ORT school in Kensington, in which Lucie was involved, was established in July 1946. See *British O.R.T. Annual Report 1946 and 1947* (London: British O.R.T., n.d.).

[47] In September 1947, Lucie was employed by 'Suzanne' Coutierre at 36 Beauchamp Pl., with a starting salary of £3.10s per week. By February 1949 her wages had risen to £4.10s. See Case file Lucie Hilsenrad, World Jewish Relief (formerly Central British Fund) Archives.

[48] Later Oscar winner Natalie Wood (1938–1981) began her career as a child star.

[49] Phoebus Tuttnauer (1890–1965), medical doctor and artist, and Olga Tuttnauer (1895–1975), physiotherapist.

[50] As early as May 1939, Jack Morrison, Lucie's and Margit's host in Glasgow, wrote to Phoebus Tuttnauer suggesting he should look after Lucie and Margit for a short holiday period. The reply was that there was no room for the girls in Tuttnauer's flat. A further letter, in which Morrison pointed out Tuttnauer's obligations to his relatives, seems to have remained unanswered. See Case file Lucie Hilsenrad, World Jewish Relief (formerly Central British Fund) Archives.

[51] In his unpublished 'Facets of my Family History', vol. 1, the chemist and historian Edward Gelles gives the following account: 'Back in

London, we enjoyed the company of Dr Phoebus Tuttnauer and his wife Olga. We often had lunch with them at their flat in Portland Place. Phoebus was born in the Austro-Hungarian province of Bukowina (later a part of Rumania). He studied medicine in Vienna, and like my father became a Zionist in his student days. His participation in the movement continued in London. He supported his wife Olga in her enterprising practice as a 'beautician' to a distinguished clientele. Her background of medical know-how enabled her to employ and purvey much appreciated home-made cosmetic products. In the 1950's Phoebus and Olga took up painting and had successful exhibitions at several London Galleries and elsewhere.' See https://archives.balliol.ox.ac.uk/Modern%20Papers/gelles/Facets%20o f%20my%20Family%20History.%20Part%201.%20%20Chapters%201 %20-%2012.pdf, accessed 1 November 2024.

[52] The manuscript reads '18 years', but this does not make sense as Lucie was already nineteen years old at the time mentioned. Moreover, the legal threshold for adulthood was twenty-one years of age at the time. The date 8 June is the date of the actual naturalisation.

[53] The registration fee was £10, for which Lucie received £5 as a loan from the Central British Fund. See Case file Lucie Hilsenrad, World Jewish Relief (formerly Central British Fund) Archives.

4. Travels and engagement (p. 29–32)

[54] An episode not mentioned in the memoir, Margit drew Lucie into the Church of the Brethren's peace work at the workshop 'Vienna peace institute', 10 July–18 August 1950. Lucie may have been invited to raise the number of local participants to three.

[55] Lucie left for Vienna in mid-May 1948. Her travel fare to Austria was paid for by refugee funds. The visit was only possible on compassionate grounds, which Lucie demonstrated to the Austrian Consulate by presenting medical certificates that documented her father's poor health. See Case file Lucie Hilsenrad, World Jewish Relief (formerly Central British Fund) Archives.

[56] From 1947 to 1951 Margit worked in Vienna for the Brethren Service Commission's relief activities (a branch of the US-based pietist Church of the Brethren). She began as a secretary, interpreter, and bookkeeper in the administrative office. In 1949 she became a secretary and interpreter in the Refugee Resettlement Program. The for-

mer programme director for Austria recalls her as follows: 'Our Vienna office administrative load became so heavy that we asked the Austrian employment bureau for a topflight secretary who could speak both English and German well. Among the candidates was Margit Hilsenrad who impressed us at once. She became our office anchor person – quiet, efficient, and perceptive. She served in this capacity until sometime after I left Austria. We never could have made it without her. Later she attended Manchester and Haverford Colleges and has now served with the World Health Organisation in Geneva for several years.' Ralph E. Schmeltzer, 'Brethren Service in Austria,' in *To Serve the Present Age: The Brethren Service Story*, ed. Donald F. Durnbaugh (Elgin, Ill.: Brethren Press, 1975), p. 178. Another chapter in this volume shows that Margit was based in Schweinfurt, Germany, from January to April 1950, selecting *Volksdeutsche* refugees (i.e., people from Eastern Europe with German ancestry) for a resettlement programme in the USA, see: Joseph B. Mow, 'The Refugee Resettlement Program,' in *To Serve the Present Age*, p. 198. From 1951 to 1954 Margit studied history, sociology and foreign languages at Manchester College, North Manchester, Indiana, USA, graduating with a B.A. ('with distinction'), and also working as a secretary to the dean. Thereafter she attended Haverford College in Haverford, Pennsylvania, USA, graduating in 1955 with an M.A. in social and technical assistance. To receive aid when emigrating to the USA for her studies, Margit registered as a Jewish survivor for the Joint Distribution Committee. Related documents show that both parents joined Margit in the USA in 1952, at a time when she already had an address at Haverford College (https://search.archives.jdc.org/multimedia%2F Documents%2FVMB_cardindex%2F31157_176236%2F31157_176236- 00126.jpg, accessed 1 November 2024). After returning to Europe, Margit worked from 1955 to 1957 as a secretary for the Brethren Service Commission in Geneva, Switzerland. In 1957 she began at WHO headquarters in Geneva as a technical assistant, first in the Maternal and Child Health Section, later in Environmental Health. By 1970, she was promoted to technical officer, working in that capacity until her early retirement in 1984. She continued to live in Geneva with her partner until her death. For unknown reasons, Lucie broke off contact entirely during the last decades of their lives, while Lucie's children kept in touch with Margit.

[57] In connection with Lucie's seeking British citizenship, an officer at the Central British Fund noted: 'Luzie reported on her visit to her

parents but felt she could never make her home again in Vienna. Future of her parents stay in Vienna uncertain and she herself felt entirely alien in that country. She is very well assimilated and would like to become a Naturalised British Subject. Her parents are also anxious for this and she has written for their consent.' This consent was given by Ludwig Hilsenrad. See Case file Lucie Hilsenrad, World Jewish Relief (formerly Central British Fund) Archives.

[58] The experience of 'little real connection […] between parents and children' was shared by many other Kindertransport children (see Baumel-Schwartz, *Never Look Back*, p. 222). It is one aspect of Fast's observation that 'The price parents paid in emotional trauma for their children's safety is […] beyond comprehension and must never be ignored', pointing to the need for further study of this subject (see Fast, *Children's Exodus*, pp. 142, 168).

[59] She left London by mid-August 1949. See Case file Lucie Hilsenrad, World Jewish Relief (formerly Central British Fund) Archives.

[60] Austrian titles; the prefix 'Ober-' indicates a superior position.

[61] Bengt Rösiö (1927–2019), Swedish diplomat and author who mentions Lucie in some of his books under the name 'Lucinda'. He described their encounter as follows: 'I went to Vienna and enrolled at the university for the autumn term of 1949 […] On a student excursion in Grinzing I met a young Jewish girl, Lucinda, and then it was mostly her and me. We went to the theatre, third row, sometimes to the cinema, sometimes to the opera, to museums when there were free days. Afterwards we would sit in a café and each order a *Tee mit Zitrone* and no one objected to the cheap intake – almost all Viennese were poor, and Vienna was a tired and ravaged city. I followed her on foot home to Leopoldstadt, the Jewish neighbourhood in the Soviet Russian district; her parents were still alive, though her father had been badly treated. Lucinda had been taken to London in time.' Bengt Rösiö, *Yrke: Diplomat* (Stockholm: Norstedt, 1988), p. 28. In a later book, he rephrased it thus: 'Vienna 1948 was the world of the Third Man, where Harry Lime's footsteps crept in the alleys between heavy baroque palaces and Anton Karas's zither sounded at dusk. *Tee mit Zitrone* at Cafe Mozart after the Opera or the Theater in der Josefstadt, third row side, with Lucinda, the Jewish woman to whom I later became engaged. Tram out to Grinzing, a fractured student life and the encounter with a city in ruins, worst in Leopoldstadt where

Lucinda's family lived.' Bengt Rösiö, *Hermelin bland katter: Ett rap-sodiskt och ganska kalejdoskopiskt collage av anteckningar, rapporter, artiklar, brev och annan skrivklåda i och utanför UD-tjänst 1947–2007* (Täby: Rösiö, 2009), p. 22. In the same book, Rösiö also mentions a family he knew in war-torn Leopoldstadt, being the only ones in the house with running water, and that among the other tenants there was a former Wehrmacht officer who had been a priosoner of war in the Soviet Union and in the last elections had voted for the Nazi Party (p. 19–20).

[62] In her travelling companion Bengt's accounts and photographs, no other girl figures. He recalled those travels as follows: 'In the spring of 1950 I was at the Sorbonne. Lucinda came and I had written enough articles for us to go to Morocco. We took a bus from Casablanca to Marrakech and then over the Atlas Mountains into the desert – this was many years before tourism started. From Tangier we took the boat over to Algeciras, and I remember the mosaic tiles in the square in Granada and the roses in Seville. Sometimes it was difficult with the bedbugs, but they didn't bother us much, and we moved on to Portugal and eventually to Toledo and El Greco. Eventually I [sic!] reached Andorra' (Rösiö, *Yrke: Diplomat*, p. 28–29). Among the recollections of this trip in Rösiö's *Hermelin bland katter*, the following illustrates the vigorous and tender sides of Lucie's personality: 'It was somewhere in Spain that we were trying to get on a night train. A toothless old porter offered to get us a seat, but we couldn't afford to pay him, and the quick-witted Lucinda managed to snatch two seats as we crowded in with our rucksacks and our fellow passengers looked at us doubtfully and asked "Matrimonio?"' (p. 21–22; meaning 'marriage') – 'One has such strange memories […] I remember one day in 1950 in a Moroccan village, sitting on the roof of a hostel with Lucinda, the young Jewish woman I was travelling with. A Moroccan maid was walking around moving dust, having a kid with her. Lucinda made a little spinning wheel out of paper and gave it to the child; we had no money to give. It took a while for the girl to realise what this was meant to be, but then she grasped it and her face lit up, the first time she had received a toy' (p. 8).

[63] Billy Klüver (1927–2004) was a Swedish electrical engineer who mainly worked in the USA and was best known for his collaboration with artists like Jean Tinguely, Robert Rauschenberg, John Cage, and

Andy Warhol, as well as for his leading role in the non-profit organisation Experiments in Art and Technology (E.A.T.).

[64] Johan Wilhelm Klüver (1901–1981) was the founder of Sälens Kur & Högfjällshotell, Sweden's first large-scale winter sports facility.

[65] Pontus Hultén (1924–2006) became director of the Museum of Modern Art in Stockholm and of the Musée National d'Art Moderne (Centre Pompidou) in Paris, and had leading roles in many other art institutions. For further background, see Charlotte Bydler, Andreas Gedin, and Johanna Ringarp (eds), *Pontus Hultén på Moderna Museet: Vittnesseminarium Södertörns högskola, 26 april 2017* (Huddinge: Södertörns högskola, 2018), = Samtidshistoriska frågor 38.

[66] Here the narrative returns to an earlier point in time, and if Bengt's suggestion that he first met Lucie in autumn 1949 is correct, then Lucie's half-year in Stockholm must have come later. According to Bengt, they were in Paris in the spring of 1950, something that accords with Lucie's narrative here. From there they travelled to Northern Africa and the Iberian Peninsula. In his memoir, Bengt recalls another trip, probably in the summer of 1951, which Lucie does not mention: 'Lucinda and I travelled down to Dalmatia. We took a train via Zagreb, and from Split we went by boat to Dubrovnik. There wasn't a tourist there at the time, and the Dubrovnik of the early fifties – Ragusa, as Lucinda's father called it – was still Dalmatian. We loved the city and one evening we saw Hamlet performed in Serbo-Croatian on the top of the city wall. We took the bus from Kotor up to Montenegro on the old dirt road, walked in Cetinje and then took the train back across Mostar and Sarajevo' (Rösiö, *Yrke: Diplomat*, p. 33).

[67] In a subsequent letter to a relative, Bengt touched upon the alienation, describing Lucie as 'a girl, an Austrian Jew, with whom I found much in common and much difference. It was the same with many people I knew at that time – they longed for security, I wanted to get away from it. We found each other in this pursuit of different goals, a community in security and in flight' (Rösiö, *Hermelin bland katter*, p. 20).

[68] In recalling his first foreign office assignment abroad, Bengt wrote the following: 'Shortly before, Koestler had published his autobiography, *Arrow in the Blue*. He wrote how one evening he came upon the bridge over the Danube Canal – the same one I used to walk home on from Leopoldstadt – and suddenly had the impulse to throw his medical textbooks into the water and break up. I realised that I had to

do the same with Lucinda, feeling that a new stage was upon me. She followed me to Bromma Airport, but we both knew we were drifting apart' (Rösiö, *Yrke: Diplomat*, p. 34).

5. Sweden in the 1950s (p. 33–34)

[69] Neighbourhood in the Swedish capital of Stockholm. Lucie officially immigrated to Sweden in November 1951.

[70] The official name of the firm was Trafik AB Grängesberg–Oxelösund (TGO); today it is simply Gränges.

[71] Cäcilie Westebbe (1925–2009), immigrated from Germany to Sweden in 1951.

[72] Skandinaviska Enskilda Banken, abbreviated SEB.

[73] The Liberian-American-Swedish Mining Company (LAMCO) was established in the 1950s upon the discovery of the Nimba iron ore body in Liberia and operated this mine until the end of the 1980s.

[74] Walter Widl (1930–2016), originally from Vienna, with an engineering degree from Germany, immigrated to Sweden in 1955.

[75] 'Miss, can you cook?'

[76] 'Mansion' probably refers to Nynäs gods, an estate in Nynäshamn that is owned by the Nobel family. It has been unexpectedly difficult to identify family member Eva Nobel.

6. Marriage (p. 35–38)

[77] 'Grandpa' (Walter's father).

[78] Gentian.

[79] Humanist.

[80] Rådhuset is the main courthouse of Stockholm.

[81] Eva Gugolz (b. 1932) and Max Gugolz (1924–1998), both immigrated from Switzerland to Sweden in 1955.

[82] Walter was four months younger than Lucie.

[83] Literally 'love cell', but the text refers to the village of Bad Liebenzell.

[84] Celsius.

[85] Grandma.

[86] 'Ester' is an iconic Swedish sketch by comedian and actor Martin Ljung (1917–2010) about visitors imposing themselves on their intended hosts.

[87] Irma Lockner (1931–2002) immigrated from Austria to Sweden in 1956, and Dieter Lockner (1928–2016) immigrated from Germany to Sweden in 1956.

[88] Dieter Lockner worked at the Isotope Division, Department of Alcohol Research, and the Department of Gynaecology at Radiumhemmet, which were all institutions within Karolinska Institutet medical university. Dieter Lockner's dissertation, *Studies on Cancer Anaemia* (Stockholm: Karolinska Institutet, 1966), was initiated by the 'father of nuclear medicine', the radiochemist and Nobel Prize laureate George de Hevesy (1885–1966), who headed the Isotope Division and with whom Lockner co-authored some articles.

7. Building a migrant family (p. 39–43)

[89] Södra barnbördshuset was a maternity hospital in Stockholm.

[90] Karolinska Institutet, Stockholm's university hospital.

[91] Gerhard Gobl (1930–2008) immigrated from Austria to Sweden in 1955.

[92] Serafen (i.e., Serafimerlasarettet) was a hopsital in Stockholm.

[93] The Stockholm department store Nordiska Kompaniet.

[94] Helmut Wagner (1934–2012) immigrated from Austria to Sweden in 1958, and Barbro Wagner (born 1933 in Stockholm). Ingarö is an island in the Stockholm archipelago, joined to the mainland by bridges.

[95] Refers to Gerhard Widl, Lucie's brother-in-law.

[96] Great-grandmother.

[97] Guesthouse.

[98] A local shop or bakery.

[99] Summer cottage.

[100] Baby food.

8. Second child and further medical experiences (p. 45–48)

[101] Stockholm South General Hospital.

[102] Karl-Johan Grenabo (1906–1998) was a leading Swedish plastic surgeon.

[103] 'Your daughter, who is lying inside there and crying.'

8. Second child and further medical experiences (p. 45–48)

[101] Stockholm South General Hospital.

[102] Karl-Johan Grenabo (1906–1998) was a leading Swedish plastic surgeon.

List of Illustrations

Sources and Literature

a) Archives

Archives of the Jewish Community of Vienna (IKG)
    General archive
    Matrikel-Amt
Austrian State Archives, Archiv der Republik,
    Sammelstelle A
    Sammelstelle II/A
    Vermögensverkehrsstelle
Municipal and Provincial Archives of Vienna
    Registration Records
    Sondergericht, A1
Scottish Jewish Archives Centre
Swedish Tax Agency
    National registry
World Health Organisation (WHO) archives
    Staff records
World Jewish Relief (formerly Central British Fund) Archives
    Kindertransport case files

b) Journals, primary literature, and websites

British O.R.T. Annual Report 1946 and 1947 (London: British O.R.T., n.d.).

Gelles, Edward, 'Facets of my Family History', vol. 1, unpublished manuscript, available at https://archives.balliol.ox.ac.uk/Modern%20Papers/gelles/Facets%20of%20my%20Family%20History.%20Part%201.%20%20Chapters%201%20-%2012.pdf, accessed 1 November 2024.

Gospel Messenger

Jewish Chronicle

Jewish Echo

Lockner, Dieter, *Studies on Cancer Anaemia*, PhD thesis (Stockholm: Karolinska Institutet, 1966).

Mow, Joseph B., 'The Refugee Resettlement Program,' *To Serve the Present Age: The Brethren Service Story*, ed. Donald F. Durnbaugh (Elgin, Ill.: Brethren Press, 1975).

'Photo of evacuees' (available at https://sjac-collection.is.ed.ac.uk//record/111212, accessed 1 November 2024).

Rösiö, Bengt, *Yrke: Diplomat* (Stockholm: Norstedt, 1988).

Rösiö, Bengt, *Hermelin bland katter: Ett rapsodiskt och ganska kalejdoskopiskt collage av anteckningar, rapporter, artiklar, brev och annan skrivklåda i och utanför UD-tjänst 1947–2007* (Täby: Rösiö, 2009).

Schmeltzer, Ralph E., 'Brethren Service in Austria,' in *To Serve the Present Age: The Brethren Service Story*, ed. Donald F. Durnbaugh (Elgin, Ill.: Brethren Press, 1975).

search.archives.jdc.org

Wiener Adreßbuch: Lehmanns Wohnungsanzeiger

www.ancestry.com

www.ernespiehouse.com

c) Literature

'Antonio Stradivari, Cremona, 1709, the "Marie Hall, Viotti"', available at https://tarisio.com/cozio-archive/property/?ID=41348, accessed 1 November 2024.

Baumel-Schwartz, Judith Tydor, *Never Look Back: The Jewish Refugee Children in Great Britain, 1938–1945* (West Lafayette, IN: Purdue University Press, 2012).

'The Birkenward' (available at https://www.skelmorlievillas.co.uk/skelmorlie-villas/the-birkenward/, accessed 1 November 2024).

Bukey, Evan Burr, *Jews and Intermarriage in Nazi Austria* (Cambridge: Cambridge University Press, 2011).

Bydler, Charlotte, Andreas Gedin, and Johanna Ringarp (eds), *Pontus Hultén på Moderna Museet: Vittnesseminarium Södertörns högskola, 26 april 2017* (Huddinge: Södertörns högskola, 2018), = Samtidshistoriska frågor 38.

Craig-Norton, Jennifer, *The Kindertransport: Contesting Memory* (Bloomington: Indiana University Press, 2019).

Exenberger, Herbert, Johann Koss, and Brigitte Ungar-Klein, *Kündigungsgrund Nichtarier: Die Vertreibung Jüdischer Mieter aus den Wiener Gemeindebauten in den Jahren 1938–1939* (Wien: Picus, 1996).

Fast, Vera K., *Children's Exodus: A History of the Kindertransport* (London: I.B. Tauris, 2011).

Flanders, Kappy and Andy Bronfman, *Sis & Pa: Our Family Album* (n.l.: author's edition, 2003).

Fritz, Patricia, '"Mischehen" in der NS-Zeit: Eine Betrachtung der Lebensformen der im Raum Wien beheimateten Eheleute einer Jüdisch–Christlichen "Mischehe" mit Ausblick auf die Leben der daraus hervorgegangenen Kinder', MA thesis (Graz: Karl-Franzens-Universität, 2018), available at https://unipub.uni-graz.at/obvugrhs/download/pdf/2679667, accessed 1 November 2024.

Gruner, Wolf, *Zwangsarbeit und Verfolgung: Österreichische Juden im NS-Staat 1938–45* (Innsbruck: Studien-Verlag, 2000).

Göllner, Renate, *Schule und Verbrechen: Die Vertreibung Jüdischer Schülerinnen und Schüler von Wiens Mittelschulen* (Frankfurt/Main: Lang, 2009).

Göpfert, Rebekka, *Der Jüdische Kindertransport von Deutschland nach England 1938/39: Geschichte und Erinnerung* (Frankfurt/Main: Campus, 1999).

Götz, Norbert, *Ungleiche Geschwister: Die Konstruktion von nationalsozialistischer Volksgemeinschaft und schwedischem Volksheim* (Nomos, Baden-Baden, 2001).

Götz, Norbert, Georgina Brewis, and Steffen Werther, *Humanitarianism in the Modern World: The Moral Economy of Famine Relief* (Cambridge: Cambridge University Press, 2020).

Hammel, Andrea, *The Kindertransport: What Really Happened* (Cambridge: Polity, 2024).

Koller-Glück, Elisabeth, 'Siegfried Charoux und das Charoux-Museum in Langenzersdorf', *Neues Museum*, no. 2 (1994).

Mentzel, Walter, 'Willi Pollak', in *Lexicon of Austrian Provenance Research* (Vienna: Commission for Provenance Research, 2019), available at https://www.lexikon-provenienzforschung.org/en/pollak-wilhelm, accessed 1 November 2024.

'Obituary: Jack Morrison', *Jewish Chronicle*, 2 Sept. 1977.

Offenberger, Ilana Fritz, *The Jews of Nazi Vienna, 1938–1945: Rescue and Destruction* (Cham: Springer, 2017).

Weindling, Paul, 'The Kindertransport from Vienna: The Children Who Came and Those Left Behind', *Jewish Historical Studies* 51 (2019).

Werner, Margot and Michael Wladika, *Die Tätigkeit der Sammelstellen* (Vienna: Oldenbourg, 2004).

Wexberg-Kubesch, Anna, *Vergiss nie, dass Du ein jüdisches Kind bist: Der Kindertransport nach England 1938/39* (Wien: Mandelbaum, 2013).

Williams, Frances, *The Forgotten Kindertransportees: The Scottish Experience* (London: Bloomsbury, 2014).

Issues of Contemporary History /
Samtidshistoriska frågor

This series is published by The Institute of Contemporary History (Samtidshistoriska institutet, SHI). The series summarizes and discusses significant historical events and contemporary issues. Edited transcripts from witness seminars, new research from the university's academic staff and conference reports are published as part of the series. Information about the series: https://bibl-app.sh.se/publicationseries/list?id=26.

Most of the titles in the series can be downloaded in full text, free of charge, from the Digital Science Archive, DiVA, http://www.diva-portal.se.

All titles in the series undergo editorial review. Some of them are published in collaboration with the Centre for Baltic and East European Studies (CBEES) at Södertörn University. Head editor and contact person for the publication series is Professor Norbert Götz, norbert.gotz@sh.se.

1. *Olof Palme i sin tid.* Ed. Kjell Östberg (2001).

2. *Kvinnorörelsen och '68.* Ed. Elisabeth Elgán (2001).

3. *Riv alla murar! Vittnesseminarier om sexliberalismen och om Pocket-tidningen R.* Ed. Lena Lennerhed (2002).

4. *Löntagarfonderna – en missad möjlighet?* Ed. Lars Ekdahl (2002).

5. *Dagens Nyheter: Minnesseminarium över Sven-Erik Larsson. Vittnesseminarium om DN och '68.* Ed. Alf W. Johansson (2003).

6. *Kvinnorna skall göra det! Den kvinnliga medborgarskolan på Fogelstad – som idé, text och historia.* Eds. Ebba Witt Brattström & Lena Lennerhed (2003).

7. *Moderaterna, marknaden och makten – svensk högerpolitik under avregleringens tid, 1976–1991.* Torbjörn Nilsson (2003).

8. *Upprorets estetik. Vittnesseminarier om kulturens politisering under 1960- och 1970-talet.* Ed. Lena Lennerhed (2005).

9. *Revolution på svenska – ett vittnesseminarium om jämställdhetens institutionalisering, politisering och expansion 1972–1976*. Ed. Anja Hirdman (2005).

10. *En högskola av ny typ? Två seminarier kring Södertörns högskolas tillkomst och utveckling*. Eds. Mari Gerdin & Kjell Östberg (2006).

11. *Hur rysk är den svenska kommunismen? Fyra bidrag om kommunism, nationalism och etnicitet*. Eds. Mari Gerdin & Kjell Östberg (2006).

12. *Ropen skalla – daghem åt alla! Vittnesseminarium om daghemskampen på 70-talet*. Eds. Mari Gerdin & Kajsa Ohrlander (2007).

13. *Makten i kanslihuset. Vittnesseminarium 16 maj 2006*. Eds. Emma Isaksson & Torbjörn Nilsson (2007).

14. *Partnerskapslagen – ett vittnesseminarium om partnerskapslagens tillkomst*. Eds. Emma Isaksson & Lena Lennerhed (2007).

15. *Vägar till makten – statsrådens och statssekreterarnas karriärvägar*. Anders Ivarsson Westerberg & Cajsa Niemann (2007).

16. *Sverige och Baltikums frigörelse. Två vittnesseminarier om storpolitik kring Östersjön 1991–1994*. Eds. Thomas Lundén & Torbjörn Nilsson (2008).

17. *Makten och trafiken i Stadshuset. Två vittnesseminarier om Stockholms kommunalpolitik*. Ed. Torbjörn Nilsson (2009).

18. *Norden runt i tvåhundra år. Jämförande studier om liberalism, konservatism och historiska myter*. Torbjörn Nilsson (2010).

19. *1989 med svenska ögon. Vittnesseminarium om Östeuropas omvandling*. Eds. Torbjörn Nilsson & Thomas Lundén (2010).

20. *Statsminister Göran Persson i samtal med Erik Fichtelius (1996–2006)*. Ed. Werner Schmidt (2011).

21. *Bortom rösträtten. Politik, kön och medborgarskap i Norden*. Eds. Lenita Freidenwall & Josefin Rönnbäck (2011).

22. *Borgerlig fyrklöver intog Rosenbad – regeringsskiftet 1991*. Eds. Torbjörn Nilsson & Anders Ivarsson Westerberg (2011).

23. *Rivstart för Sverige – Alliansen och maktskiftet 2006*. Eds. Fredrik Eriksson & Anders Ivarsson Westerberg (2012).

24. *Det började i Polen – Sverige och Solidaritet 1980–1981*. Ed. Fredrik Eriksson (2013).

25. *Förnyelse eller förfall? Svenska försvaret efter kalla kriget*. Ed. Fredrik Eriksson (2013).

26. *Staten och granskningssamhället.* Eds. Bengt Jacobsson & Anders Ivarsson Westerberg (2013).

27. *Almedalen – varför är vi här? Så skapades en politikens marknadsplats – Ett vittnesseminarium om Almedalsveckan som politisk arena.* Ed. Kjell Östberg (2013).

28. *Anarkosyndikalismens återkomst i Spanien. SACs samarbete med CNT under övergången från diktatur till demokrati.* Ed. Per Lindblom (2014).

29. *När blev vården marknad? Vittnesseminarium i Almedalen.* Ed. Kristina Abiala (2014).

30. *Brinner "förorten"? Om sociala konflikter i Botkyrka och Huddinge.* Ed. Kristina Abiala (2014).

31. *Sea of Identities: A Century of Baltic and East European Experiences with Nationality, Class, and Gender.* Ed. Norbert Götz (2014).

32. *När räntan gick i taket: Vittnesseminarium om valutakrisen 1992.* Ed. Cecilia Åse (2015).

33. *Nordiskt samarbete i kalla krigets kölvatten. Vittnesseminarium med Uffe Ellemann-Jensen, Mats Hellström och Pär Stenbäck.* Eds. Johan Strang & Norbert Götz (2016).

34. *Solidariteten med Chile 1973–1989.* Eds. Yulia Gradskova & Monica Quirico (2016).

35. *25 år av skolreformer – hur började det? Vittnesseminarium om skolans kommunalisering och friskolereformen.* Ed. Johanna Ringarp (2017).

36. *Levande campus: Utmaningar och möjligheter för Södertörns högskola i den nya regionala stadskärnan i Flemingsberg.* Eds. Johanna Ringarp & Håkan Forsell (2017).

37. *Utbildningsvetenskap: Vittnesseminarium om ett vetenskapsområdes uppkomst, utveckling och samtida utmaningar.* Eds. Anders Burman, Daniel Lövheim & Johanna Ringarp (2018).

38. *Pontus Hultén på Moderna Museet: Vittnesseminarium på Södertörns högskola, 26 april 2017.* Eds. Charlotte Bydler, Andreas Gedin & Johanna Ringarp (2018).

39. *AIDS i Sverige: Hivepidemin och rörelserna.* Eds. Kjell Östberg & Lena Lennerhed (2019).

40. *Romerna och skolplikten: Hot eller möjlighet?* Ed. Håkan Blomqvist (2020).

41. *Sweden in Solidarity, Museums in Exile: The Chilean Resistance Museum in Solidarity with Salvador Allende and the International Art Exhibition for Palestine*. Ed. Charlotte Bydler (2022).

42. *Kamp mot droger: En bok om Förbundet mot droger*. Kjell Östberg (2019).

43. *North and South: European Social Democracy in the 1970s*. Eds. Alan Granadino, Carl Marklund & Johan Strang (2021).

44. *Recollections of Joining the EU: Iberian and Nordic Experiences*. Eds. Alan Granadino, Peter Stadius & Carl Marklund (2023).

45. *Visions of the Nordic Model in Northern and Southern Europe (1970s–1990s)*. Eds. Alan Granadino, Andreas Mørkved Hellenes & Carl Marklund (2023).

46. *Sverigebilden i USA: Historia, händelser och mekanismer*. Carl Marklund (2023).

47. *The Image of Sweden in the USA: History, Events and Mechanisms*. Carl Marklund (2024).

48. *Biafra and the Nordic Media: Witness Seminar with Uno Grönkvist, Lasse Jensen, Pierre Mens, and Pekka Peltola*. Eds. Norbert Götz & Carl Marklund (2024).

49. *Nejlikerevolutionen och den svenska Portugal-solidariteten 1974–1981*. Jan Olsson (ed. Carl Marklund) (2024).

50. *From Kindertransport to Post-war Sweden: My Memories*. Lucie Widl (ed. Norbert Götz) (2025).